Navigating the First Year as a Modern Grandparent

A Comprehensive Guide

Charlotte Anderson

© **Copyright 2024 - All rights reserved.**

The content contained within this book may not be reproduced, duplicated or transmitted without direct written permission from the author or the publisher.

Under no circumstances will any blame or legal responsibility be held against the publisher, or author, for any damages, reparation, or monetary loss due to the information contained within this book, either directly or indirectly.

Legal Notice:

This book is copyright protected. It is only for personal use. You cannot amend, distribute, sell, use, quote or paraphrase any part, or the content within this book, without the consent of the author or publisher.

Disclaimer Notice:

Please note the information contained within this document is for educational and entertainment purposes only. All effort has been executed to present accurate, up to date, reliable, complete information. No warranties of any kind are declared or implied. Readers acknowledge that the author is not engaged in the rendering of legal, financial, medical or professional advice. The content within this book has been derived from various sources. Please consult a licensed professional before attempting any techniques outlined in this book.

By reading this document, the reader agrees that under no circumstances is the author responsible for any losses, direct or indirect, that are incurred as a result of the use of the information contained within this document, including, but not limited to, errors, omissions, or inaccuracies.

Table of Contents

INTRODUCTION: THE GRAND ADVENTURE BEGINS 1

CHAPTER 1: EMBRACING YOUR NEW ROLE 7

THE EMOTIONAL TRANSITION: FROM PARENT TO GRANDPARENT 7
- Joy and Excitement 7
- Nostalgia 8
- Anxiety and Uncertainty 10
- Managing Your Emotions 11
- Adapting to Your New Role 12

SETTING EXPECTATIONS: NAVIGATING NEW FAMILY DYNAMICS 13
- The Importance of Open Communication 13
- Starting the Conversation 14
- Real-Life Examples of Successful Expectation-Setting 16

FINDING YOUR GRANDPARENTING STYLE 18
EXPLORING DIFFERENT GRANDPARENTING STYLES 19
- Self-Assessment Quiz: Finding Your Grandparenting Style 21
- Adapting Your Style 24

CHAPTER 2: BUILDING A STRONG RELATIONSHIP WITH YOUR GRANDCHILD 27

BUILDING A STRONG RELATIONSHIP WITH YOUR GRANDCHILD 27
CREATING MEMORABLE MOMENTS 31
- When creating traditions, keep in mind: 35
THE IMPORTANCE OF PLAYTIME 37

CHAPTER 3: GETTING AROUND THE LATEST PARENTING TRENDS 43

THE ROLE OF TECHNOLOGY IN MODERN PARENTING 43
- Digital Parenting Tools and Applications 43
- Social Media and Parenting 45
- Staying Connected as a Grandparent 46
- Balancing Technology and Traditional Parenting 47

UPDATES ON HEALTH AND SAFETY GUIDELINES 48
- Nutrition Guidelines 49
- Sleep Safety 50
- Car Seat Safety 51
- Staying Updated on Guidelines 52

    CONTEMPORARY PARENTING PHILOSOPHIES 53
        Attachment Parenting 54
        Montessori Parenting 55
        Positive Parenting 56
        Supporting Different Parenting Philosophies 58

CHAPTER 4: LONG-DISTANCE GRANDPARENTING: NURTURING CONNECTIONS ACROSS MILES 61

    THE VIRTUAL WAY: MAXIMIZING DIGITAL CONNECTIONS 61
        Making the Most of Video Calls 62
        Interactive Activities for Virtual Visits 63
    CREATIVE COMMUNICATION: BEYOND VIDEO CALLS 66
        The Power of Letters and Emails 66
        Care Packages: Sending Love in a Box 68
        Making Visit Plans: Maximizing In-Person Time 70
    PLANNING ENJOYABLE AND HASSLE-FREE VISITS 71
        Communicate Clearly with the Parents 71
        Plan Activities in Advance 72
        Respect Household Rules 73
        Honoring Parents' Routines and Boundaries 74
        Stick to Established Routines 74
        Ask Before Giving Treats or Gifts 74
        Respect Parenting Decisions 75
        Offer Support Without Criticism 75
        Making the Most of Limited In-Person Time 76

CHAPTER 5: BALANCING GRANDPARENTING WITH PERSONAL LIFE 79

        The Importance of Personal Well-being and Self-care 79
        Practical Self-care Routines and Activities 80
        The Impact of Physical and Emotional Wellness on Grandparenting 82
        Balancing Act: Strategies for Harmony 83
    PURSUING HOBBIES AND INTERESTS 84
        Balancing Grandparenting and Personal Passions 84
        Integrating Grandchildren into Personal Activities 86
    SETTING BOUNDARIES 89
        The Importance of Boundaries 90
        Strategies for Communicating Boundaries 91

CHAPTER 6: SUPPORTING NEW PARENTS 97
   Offering Practical Support 97
   Being Present Without Dominating 98
   Small Gestures That Make a Big Difference 99
   Creating a Supportive Environment 100
   Adapting to Modern Parenting Practices 101
  HONORING PARENTAL DECISIONS 102
   Respecting Parenting Choices 102
   Dealing with Divergent Parenting Ideologies 104
   Examples of Considerate and Encouraging Grandparents 105
  IMPROVING COMMUNICATION 108
   The Importance of Open and Honest Communication 108
   Techniques for Having Difficult Conversations 109
   Effective Communication Strategies 110
   Special Circumstances: Supporting Parents of NICU Babies 112

CHAPTER 7: ESTABLISHING A NETWORK OF GRANDPARENTS 115
   The Benefits of Connecting with Other Grandparents 115
   Finding and Joining Grandparent Groups 118
  SHARING RESOURCES AND COLLECTIVE WISDOM 121
   Exchanging Tips and Activities 122
   The Value of Shared Experiences 123
   Recommended Resources 124
  ORGANIZING GATHERINGS FOR GRANDPARENTS 126
   Creating a Welcoming Atmosphere 126
   Planning Engaging Activities 128
   Organizing Multigenerational Events 130

CHAPTER 8: LEAVING A LEGACY 133
   The Importance of Family Traditions and Tales 133
   Creating Family History Books and Videos 134
   Examples of Meaningful Family Legacies 136
  TEACHING VALUES AND LIFE LESSONS 138
   The Role of Grandparents in Imparting Wisdom 138
   Methods for Imparting Life Lessons 140
   Stories of Influential Grandparents 142
  CREATING LASTING MEMORIES 144
   The Value of Shared Experiences 144
   The Impact on Growth and Emotions 145

CONCLUSION **147**

GLOSSARY **151**

REFERENCES **155**

Introduction:

The Grand Adventure Begins

Picture this: You're standing in the hospital corridor, heart racing, palms sweaty. The anticipation builds as you wait for news of your grandchild's arrival. Suddenly, the door swings open, and your adult child emerges, beaming with joy. "It's a girl!" they exclaim, and just like that, your world shifts on its axis. You're a grandparent now, and a whole new chapter of life unfolds before you.

That was me, Charlotte Anderson, on a sunny Tuesday morning in June as I held my tiny granddaughter for the first time; a whirlwind of emotions swept over me. Joy, love, and excitement mingled with a touch of anxiety and uncertainty. How would I navigate this new role? What kind of grandmother did I want to be? And most importantly, how could I support my children while respecting their parenting choices?

If you're reading this, chances are you're embarking on a similar journey. Whether you're a soon-to-be grandparent or you've recently joined the grandparent club, welcome! You're about to embark on one of life's most rewarding adventures. But let's be honest, it's not always smooth sailing. The world of parenting has changed dramatically since we raised our own children, and the role of grandparents has evolved along with it.

That's where this book comes in. Consider it your friendly guide to modern grandparenting, packed with practical advice, heartwarming stories, and a healthy dose of humor. We'll navigate the exciting (and sometimes choppy) waters of first-year grandparenting together, tackling everything from building strong relationships with your grandchildren to mastering the art of long-distance bonding.

Throughout these pages, we'll explore:

- Embracing Your New Role: We'll dive into the emotional rollercoaster of becoming a grandparent and help you find your unique grandparenting style. As Chandler Bolt notes in his guide on writing book introductions, "The key is to connect with your reader's emotions and needs right from the start" (Bolt, 2020).

- Building Strong Bonds: Discover fun and meaningful ways to connect with your grandchild, even if you live far apart. We'll cover everything from playtime activities to creating lasting traditions.

- Navigating Modern Parenting Trends: Get up to speed on the latest parenting philosophies, health guidelines, and technologies. Don't worry; we'll break it all down in easy-to-understand terms.

- Supporting New Parents: Learn how to be a valuable support system for your adult children without overstepping boundaries. It's a delicate balance, but we'll show you how to master it.

- Finding Your Grandparent Tribe: Connect with other grandparents and build a supportive network. After all, it takes a village to raise a child – and support a grandparent!

- Leaving a Legacy: Discover meaningful ways to pass down family history, values, and traditions to future generations.

Now, I know what you might be thinking. "Charlotte, this all sounds great, but I'm nervous about messing up or saying the wrong thing." Trust me, I've been there. In fact, let me share a quick story that might make you feel better.

On my first solo babysitting adventure with my grandson, I was determined to be the perfect grandmother. I had a day of educational activities planned, organic snacks prepared, and a diaper bag packed with military precision. Everything was going smoothly until naptime rolled around. As I gently laid her in the crib, I realized with horror that I had no idea how to operate the new-fangled baby monitor. After 15 minutes of frantic button-pushing and mild panic, I resigned myself to sitting by the crib for the entire nap, terrified I'd miss her waking up. When my daughter returned home to find me, bleary-eyed and stiff-necked, camped out in the nursery, we shared a good laugh. It was a humbling reminder that perfection isn't the goal – love, effort, and a good sense of humor are what really matter.

This book is filled with similar stories from grandparents who've been in your shoes. We'll laugh together, learn together, and celebrate the joys and challenges of modern grandparenting. As Barrie Davenport advises in her guide to writing book introductions, "Share your own experiences and vulnerabilities. This helps readers relate to you and trust your advice" (Davenport, 2023).

So, grab a cup of tea (or something stronger – no judgment here), settle into your favorite chair, and let's embark on this grand adventure together. By the time you finish this book, you'll be armed with the knowledge, confidence, and enthusiasm to rock your new role as a modern grandparent. Remember, there's no one "right" way to be a grandparent. Your journey will be as unique as you are. But with a little guidance, a lot of love, and a healthy dose of flexibility, you're in for the ride of a lifetime. Are you ready? Let's dive in!

But before we do, let's take a moment to address the elephant in the room – the vast differences between grandparenting today and when we were raising our own children. The world has changed dramatically, and so has the role of grandparents. Gone are the days when grandma and grandpa were simply occasional babysitters or holiday visitors. Today's grandparents are often deeply involved in their grandchildren's lives, providing everything from childcare to financial support.

According to a study by the American Association of Retired Persons (AARP), nearly half of all grandparents in the United States provide some form of childcare for their grandchildren (AARP, 2018). This shift has brought both opportunities and challenges. On one hand, it allows for closer relationships and more frequent interactions with our grandchildren. On the other, it can sometimes blur the lines between parenting and grandparenting, leading to potential conflicts with our adult children.

But don't worry – we'll tackle these challenges head-on throughout this book. We'll explore ways to navigate these new waters while maintaining healthy boundaries and fostering positive relationships with both our grandchildren and their parents. One of the most significant changes in modern grandparenting is the role of technology. When we were raising our children, the internet was in its infancy, and smartphones were the stuff of science fiction. Now, they're an integral part of daily life, even for the youngest members of our families. As grandparents, we need to adapt to this new digital landscape.

This might seem daunting at first, but I promise you, it's not as scary as it seems. In fact, technology can be a wonderful tool for grandparents, especially those who live far from their grandchildren. Video calls, messaging apps, and social media platforms can help us stay connected and involved in our grandchildren's lives, even when we can't be there in person. We'll dedicate an entire chapter to mastering these digital tools, so even if you're not tech-savvy now, you will be by the time you finish this book! Another crucial aspect of modern grandparenting that we'll explore is the changing landscape of family structures. Today's families come in all shapes and sizes – blended families, single-parent families, same-sex parent families, and more. As grandparents, it's our job to embrace and support these diverse family structures, providing love and acceptance for all our grandchildren, regardless of how they came into our lives.

We'll also delve into the important topic of cultural sensitivity. In our increasingly globalized world, many families are multicultural, and grandparents play a crucial role in helping children understand and appreciate their diverse heritage. Whether you're navigating different cultural traditions, languages, or religions, we'll provide you with tools and strategies to celebrate diversity and foster a rich, multicultural family environment.

Now, let's talk about one of the most rewarding aspects of grandparenting – the opportunity to pass down family history and traditions. In our fast-paced, technology-driven world, grandparents often serve as the keepers of family lore and the bridge between past and present. We'll explore creative ways to share your family's story with your grandchildren, from creating digital scrapbooks to recording oral histories. These shared stories and traditions can help create a sense of belonging and identity for your grandchildren, giving them roots in an ever-changing world.

But being a modern grandparent isn't just about looking back – it's also about staying current and engaged with the world around us. We'll discuss the importance of lifelong learning and how sharing your passions and interests with your grandchildren can create strong bonds and inspire their own curiosity about the world. Throughout this book, we'll also address some of the more challenging aspects of grandparenting. What do you do when you disagree with your children's parenting choices? How can you maintain your own life and interests while being an involved grandparent? What if you're suddenly thrust into the role of primary caregiver for your grandchildren? These are complex issues that many grandparents face, and we'll tackle them with honesty, empathy, and practical advice.

Remember, this book isn't about telling you there's only one "right" way to be a grandparent. Instead, it's about providing you with the tools, knowledge, and confidence to find your own path. Every family is unique, and what works for one may not work for another. The key is to approach your role with love, flexibility, and open communication.

As we embark on this journey together, I want you to know that it's okay to feel overwhelmed at times. Becoming a grandparent is a major life transition, and like all big changes, it comes with its share of challenges. But it also brings immeasurable joy, love, and fulfillment. The bond between a grandparent and grandchild is truly special – it's a relationship built on unconditional love, free from the day-to-day responsibilities of parenting.

So, as you turn these pages, remember that you're not alone in this journey. Millions of grandparents around the world are navigating these same waters, and we're all learning as we go. This book is your companion, your guide, and your cheerleader as you embrace this wonderful new chapter in your life.

Are you ready to dive into the world of modern grandparenting? To learn, grow, and discover the joys that await you? To create memories that will last a lifetime and leave a legacy of love for generations to come? Then, let's begin this grand adventure together. Turn the page, and let's explore the wonderful world of grandparenting in the 21st century!

Chapter 1:

Embracing Your New Role

The moment you first hold your grandchild in your arms, your world changes forever. As you gaze into those tiny eyes, a rush of emotions washes over you - joy, love, excitement, and perhaps a touch of anxiety. Welcome to grandparenthood, a role that will challenge, delight, and transform you in ways you never imagined.

The Emotional Transition: From Parent to Grandparent

Becoming a grandparent is a significant life transition that brings with it a complex mix of emotions. As you embark on this new journey, it's essential to acknowledge and embrace these feelings.

Joy and Excitement

The moment you first lay eyes on your newborn grandchild, an indescribable wave of emotion washes over you. It's a feeling that's hard to put into words, but many grandparents describe it as pure, unadulterated joy. This happiness is unlike anything you've experienced before - even different from when you became a parent yourself.

As I held my first granddaughter, Sophia, I was struck by the intensity of my feelings. My heart felt like it might burst with love, and I couldn't stop the tears of joy from flowing. It was as if all the worries and stresses of daily life melted away, leaving only this perfect moment of connection with this tiny, precious being.

Maria, a grandmother of three, beautifully captures this sentiment: "The love you have for your grandchildren is different from any other love. It's like your heart grows a whole new chamber just for them" (Johnson, 2023). Her words resonate deeply with my own experience. It's as if nature has designed us to feel this overwhelming surge of love and protectiveness for our grandchildren.

What makes this joy so special is its purity. As grandparents, we're often spared the exhaustion and anxiety that new parents face. We don't have to worry about midnight feedings or diaper changes (unless we choose to help). Instead, we can focus entirely on the wonder and delight of this new life.

I remember watching my daughter and son-in-law in those early days with Sophia. They were sleep-deprived and overwhelmed but still so in love with their baby. As a grandparent, I had the luxury of swooping in, showering Sophia with love and attention, and then handing her back when she needed feeding or changing. It allowed me to experience all the joy of a newborn without the stress and responsibility of being the primary caregiver.

Nostalgia

As the years pass and you witness your children embark on their own parenting journeys, a profound sense of nostalgia often washes over you. This bittersweet emotion catches you off guard, transporting you back to the days when you were a new parent, filled with a mix of excitement, anxiety, and overwhelming love. Memories cascade through your mind like a montage of cherished moments. You recall the first time you held your child, their tiny fingers wrapping around yours, and the indescribable feeling of unconditional love that flooded your heart. The sleepless nights, the first smiles, the wobbly first steps - all these experiences rush back with startling clarity.

You find yourself smiling as you remember the little quirks and habits your children had as toddlers. The way they mispronounced certain words, their favorite bedtime stories, and the seemingly endless energy that kept them bouncing off the walls. These memories, once daily occurrences, now feel like precious gems you want to hold onto forever.

There's a bittersweetness to this nostalgia, too. You might feel a pang of sadness as you realize how quickly time has passed. The babies you once cradled are now adults, starting families of their own. You may find yourself wishing you could turn back the clock, if only for a moment, to relive those magical early years.

However, this nostalgia serves a beautiful purpose. It becomes a bridge between past and present, allowing you to connect with your children on a deeper level as they step into their new roles as parents. You can share your experiences, both the joys and the challenges, offering guidance and support rooted in your own journey.

As you watch your children navigate the ups and downs of parenthood, you'll likely see echoes of your own experiences. This creates a unique opportunity for bonding and understanding. Your nostalgia becomes a valuable tool, helping you empathize with their struggles and celebrate their triumphs.

Anxiety and Uncertainty

Becoming a grandparent is often portrayed as a joyous, carefree experience. While it certainly brings immense happiness, many new grandparents find themselves grappling with unexpected feelings of anxiety and uncertainty. These emotions, though rarely discussed openly, are a common and natural part of stepping into this new role.

As you embark on this journey, you might find yourself lying awake at night, mind racing with worries and questions. "Am I overstepping my boundaries?" "What if I'm not up-to-date with modern parenting practices?" "Will I be 'good enough' as a grandparent?" These concerns can feel overwhelming, but it's important to recognize that you're not alone in experiencing them.

John, a first-time grandfather, shared his experience: "I was terrified of doing something wrong. The world of parenting seemed to have changed so much since I raised my own kids. I worried about using outdated techniques or giving advice that would clash with my daughter's parenting style. It kept me up at night, honestly."

This anxiety often stems from a deep desire to be the best possible grandparent. You want to support your children, bond with your grandchildren, and create lasting memories. But the fear of making mistakes or being seen as out-of-touch can be paralyzing. You might find yourself second-guessing every interaction, wondering if you're doing it "right."

Modern parenting practices have indeed evolved rapidly. From sleep training methods to dietary guidelines, what was considered best practice when you were a parent might now be outdated. This reality can leave you feeling uncertain about your role and the value of your experience.

Moreover, the dynamics of family relationships shift when grandchildren enter the picture. You're no longer the primary decision-maker for a child's upbringing. Learning to step back and respect your adult children's parenting choices can be a challenging adjustment, often leading to feelings of anxiety about overstepping boundaries.

However, as John discovered, these initial fears often give way to a beautiful realization. "After a few weeks of tiptoeing around, I finally opened up to my daughter about my concerns," he said. "To my surprise, she was relieved. She told me she had been worried about living up to my expectations as a parent! We had a great talk, and I soon realized that love and patience were the most important things I could offer."

Managing Your Emotions

To fully embrace your new role, it's crucial to manage these emotions effectively:

- **Acknowledge your feelings:** Allow yourself to experience the full spectrum of emotions without judgment.

- **Share your thoughts:** Talk to your partner, friends, or other grandparents about what you're feeling. You'll likely find that many share similar experiences.

- **Practice mindfulness:** Stay present in the moment, savoring the joys of grandparenthood without getting too caught up in worries about the future.

- **Keep a journal:** Writing about your experiences and emotions can be a therapeutic way to process this new chapter in your life.

- **Seek support if needed:** If you're struggling with overwhelming emotions, don't hesitate to seek professional help.

Adapting to Your New Role

Stepping into the role of a grandparent is a transformative experience, one that brings joy, challenges, and unexpected revelations. It's a journey that requires flexibility, patience, and a willingness to learn and grow. As many seasoned grandparents will tell you, adapting to this new role is not a one-time event but an ongoing process filled with moments of delight, humility, and self-discovery.

Sarah, a 62-year-old grandmother of two, shares her experience with a mixture of amusement and wisdom. "I thought I knew everything about babies after raising three kids," she says with a chuckle. "But when my granddaughter arrived, I realized how much things had changed in just a generation. Suddenly, I was faced with new feeding schedules, sleep training methods, and safety guidelines I'd never heard of before."

Sarah's initial confidence quickly gave way to a humbling realization. "I had to learn to step back and let my daughter take the lead, even when it was hard," she admits. "There were times when I wanted to jump in with advice or do things the way I always had, but I had to remind myself that this wasn't my child to raise."

This adjustment wasn't always easy for Sarah. She recalls moments of frustration when her daughter chose parenting methods different from her own. "But you know what?" she says, "Those challenges actually made our relationship stronger. We learned to communicate more openly, and I gained a deeper respect for my daughter as a mother."

Tom, a 58-year-old grandfather, had a different set of concerns when he first learned he was going to be a grandpa. "I was worried about being an 'old' grandpa," he confesses. "I pictured myself sitting in a rocking chair, too tired to play or keep up with a young child."

However, Tom's experience turned out to be quite different from what he imagined. "My energy levels skyrocketed when my grandson came along," he says with evident joy. "Suddenly, I was on the floor playing with blocks and chasing him around the park. It's like being a parent again but with all the fun and none of the sleepless nights!"

Setting Expectations: Navigating New Family Dynamics

As you embark on the exciting journey of grandparenthood, one of the most crucial steps you'll take is establishing clear expectations with your adult children and their partners. This process, while sometimes challenging, is the bedrock upon which harmonious family relationships are built. It's not just about avoiding conflicts; it's about creating a framework that allows your role as a grandparent to flourish while respecting the boundaries and wishes of the new parents.

The Importance of Open Communication

Open, honest communication is more than just a nice-to-have in family dynamics; it's an absolute necessity, especially when navigating the complex waters of intergenerational relationships. As the renowned psychologist Dr. Henry Cloud wisely states, "Clear is kind. Unclear is unkind." This principle is particularly pertinent when it comes to grandparenting.

When expectations are left unspoken, they become a breeding ground for misunderstandings, hurt feelings, and resentment. On the other hand, clear communication fosters an environment of mutual respect and understanding. It allows everyone involved to express their needs, concerns, and desires openly, leading to a more harmonious family dynamic.

Consider, for instance, the frequency of visits. Without clear communication, a grandparent might assume they're welcome to drop by anytime, while the new parents might feel overwhelmed by unexpected visits. By discussing this openly, both parties can arrive at a mutually agreeable arrangement that respects the parents' need for space while ensuring the grandparents have ample opportunity to bond with their grandchild.

Moreover, open communication sets a positive example for the younger generation. It demonstrates healthy relationship skills that your grandchildren will observe and, hopefully, emulate in their own lives as they grow older.

Starting the Conversation

Initiating discussions about expectations can indeed feel daunting. Many grandparents worry about coming across as overbearing or, conversely, as disinterested. However, remember that your adult children are likely just as anxious about these conversations. They may be wrestling with how to assert their parenting choices while still honoring your experience and desire to be involved.

To help navigate this potentially tricky terrain, consider the following tips to get the conversation flowing:

- **Choose the right time:** Timing is crucial when it comes to these important discussions. Look for a moment when everyone involved is relaxed and not rushed. This might be during a family dinner, a weekend visit, or even a planned meeting specifically for this purpose. Avoid times of high stress, such as right after the baby is born or during major life transitions.

- **Use "I" statements:** The way you phrase your thoughts can significantly impact how they're received. Using "I" statements helps express your feelings and desires without sounding accusatory or demanding. For example, instead of saying, "You should let me babysit more often," try, "I would love to spend more one-on-one time with my grandchild. How do you feel about me babysitting occasionally?"

- **Listen actively:** Active listening is a skill that's often overlooked but is crucial in these conversations. Pay close attention to your children's wishes and concerns without interrupting or becoming defensive. Show that you're listening by nodding, maintaining eye contact, and asking clarifying questions. This demonstrates respect for their viewpoint and helps build trust.

- **Be open to compromise:** Remember, this conversation is not a negotiation where there are winners and losers. It's a collaborative process aimed at finding solutions that work for everyone. Be prepared to compromise and find a middle ground. For instance, if you want to see your grandchild every weekend, but the parents prefer monthly visits, perhaps you could agree on bi-weekly visits or a mix of in-person and video calls.

- **Respect boundaries:** It's crucial to acknowledge and respect that your adult children are now the primary decision-makers for their family. This can be a difficult adjustment, especially if you're used to being the one in charge. However, showing respect for their boundaries will go a long way in fostering a positive relationship.

Real-Life Examples of Successful Expectation-Setting

While every family is unique, learning from others who have successfully navigated these waters can provide valuable insights. Let's delve deeper into a couple of real-life examples:

The Johnson Family:

Linda Johnson's experience offers a great example of proactive communication. "When our first grandchild was on the way, we sat down with our daughter and son-in-law," she recalls. "We discussed everything from how often we'd visit to our stance on giving unsolicited advice. It wasn't always easy, but that conversation set the tone for a respectful and loving relationship."

The Johnsons' approach demonstrates the value of addressing potential issues before they arise. By discussing visit frequency, they avoided the awkwardness of unexpected drop-ins or feelings of neglect. Addressing the topic of unsolicited advice head-on was particularly wise. Many new parents struggle with well-meaning but overwhelming input from grandparents. By agreeing on how and when advice would be offered, the Johnsons created a framework that respected the new parents' autonomy while still allowing for the sharing of valuable experience.

Linda adds, "We also talked about our role during visits. We made it clear that we were there to support, not to take over. This meant offering to do household chores or watch the baby, so our daughter could nap, rather than swooping in and changing established routines."

This conversation wasn't a one-time event for the Johnsons. They made a point of checking in regularly, adjusting their approach as their grandchild grew and the family's needs evolved. This flexibility and ongoing communication have been key to maintaining their harmonious relationship.

The Garcia Family:

The experience of the Garcia family offers insight into managing expectations when living in close proximity to grandchildren. Carlos Garcia shares, "We live close to our son and his family, and we wanted to be involved without overstepping. We agreed on a weekly family dinner and offered to babysit one afternoon a week. This routine has given us quality time with our grandkids while respecting our son's parenting space."

The Garcias' approach illustrates the importance of finding a balance between involvement and independence. By establishing a regular schedule, they created predictability that benefited everyone. The weekly dinner provided a consistent opportunity for family bonding, while the set babysitting time allowed the parents to plan around it and the grandparents to have one-on-one time with their grandchildren.

Carlos elaborates, "We also discussed how to handle last-minute requests or changes to the schedule. We agreed that it was okay for either party to reschedule if needed as long as we gave each other as much notice as possible. This flexibility has been crucial in maintaining our arrangement without it becoming a source of stress."

The Garcias also made a point of discussing their role during emergencies or when the parents are away. "We wanted to be clear about when we might be called upon for extended childcare and what that would entail," Carlos explains. "This included discussing any dietary restrictions, discipline approaches, and daily routines we should follow to maintain consistency for the kids."

These real-life examples illustrate how clear communication and mutual respect can lead to positive outcomes for all family members. They show that with open dialogue, flexibility, and a willingness to compromise, families can create arrangements that allow grandparents to be deeply involved in their grandchildren's lives while respecting the parents' primary role.

Finding Your Grandparenting Style

Just as every grandparent is unique, with their own personalities, life experiences, and values, so too are grandparenting styles. The way you approach your role as a grandparent will be a reflection of who you are, your relationship with your adult children, and the needs of your grandchildren. Finding an approach that aligns with your personality, values, and family dynamics is key to feeling comfortable and confident in your new role. This process of discovering your grandparenting style is not just about fitting into a predetermined category but about exploring what feels natural to you and what works best for your family.

Exploring Different Grandparenting Styles

Researchers in family dynamics and child development have identified several common grandparenting styles. These categories provide a helpful framework for understanding different approaches, but it's important to remember that they are not rigid classifications. Many grandparents find that they naturally blend aspects of different styles or that their approach evolves over time.

Let's delve deeper into these common grandparenting styles:

- **Formal:** These grandparents maintain a degree of authority and may be more involved in discipline. They often see their role as an extension of their parenting years, providing structure and guidance to their grandchildren. Formal grandparents might be more likely to enforce rules and expectations, viewing their role as one of mentor and teacher.
  - For example, a formal grandparent might have set routines when their grandchildren visit, such as specific mealtimes or designated quiet hours for reading or homework. They may also be more likely to offer advice on behavior and manners.

- **Fun-Seeker:** These grandparents focus on entertainment and enjoyment with their grandchildren. They often see their role as being the "fun" adult in their grandchildren's lives, free from the responsibilities of day-to-day parenting. Fun-seeker grandparents might be more likely to plan exciting outings, indulge in treats, or bend the rules a bit for the sake of creating joyful memories.

o A fun-seeker grandparent might be the one to suggest a spontaneous trip to the ice cream parlor, organize backyard camping adventures, or have a special stash of toys and games that only come out when the grandchildren visit.

- **Distant:** Often, due to geographical separation, these grandparents have less frequent but still meaningful interactions. While they may not be present for day-to-day activities, distant grandparents often put extra effort into making their time together special and staying connected through technology.

   o A distant grandparent might schedule regular video calls, send care packages or letters, and plan extended visits during holidays or summer vacations. They might also make an effort to learn about their grandchildren's interests and friends to stay connected despite the physical distance.

- **Surrogate Parent:** These grandparents take on significant caregiving responsibilities. This might be due to various circumstances, such as the parents' work schedules, health issues, or other family situations. Surrogate parent grandparents often play a crucial role in their grandchildren's daily lives, providing stability and support.

   o A surrogate parent or grandparent might be responsible for school pick-ups and drop-offs, help with homework, prepare meals, and be involved in medical appointments and extracurricular activities. They often work closely with the parents to ensure consistency in care and discipline.

- **Reservoir of Family Wisdom:** These grandparents serve as the keepers of family history and traditions. They often see their role as passing down cultural heritage, family stories, and life lessons to the younger generation. These grandparents might be more likely to engage in activities that connect their grandchildren to their roots and heritage.

    o A reservoir of family wisdom, grandparents might spend time teaching grandchildren about their ancestry, sharing old photographs and heirlooms, cooking traditional family recipes together, or passing down skills like woodworking or needlecraft.

Remember, these categories are not rigid, and many grandparents blend aspects of different styles. Your approach may also vary depending on the age of your grandchildren, your relationship with their parents, and other family circumstances.

Self-Assessment Quiz: Finding Your Grandparenting Style

To help you identify your natural grandparenting style, consider the following questions. Take some time to reflect on each one, considering not just your immediate response but also the reasons behind your answer.

How often do you envision spending time with your grandchildren?

a) As often as possible

b) On a regular, scheduled basis

c) For special occasions and holidays

d) Whenever I'm needed

Think about your ideal level of involvement. Do you want to be a daily presence in your grandchildren's lives, or do you prefer to have special, dedicated time together? Consider your own schedule, energy levels, and other commitments.

What kind of activities do you most look forward to doing with your grandchildren?

a) Educational activities like reading or museum visits

b) Outdoor adventures and sports

c) Arts and crafts

d) Sharing family stories and traditions

Reflect on your own interests and skills. What brings you joy, and what would you like to share with your grandchildren? Remember that different activities might appeal to you as your grandchildren grow and their interests evolve.

How do you feel about discipline?

a) I believe in firm discipline and clear rules

b) I prefer to leave discipline to the parents

c) I believe in gentle guidance rather than strict discipline

d) I'm comfortable enforcing the parents' rules when babysitting

This can be a sensitive topic, so it's important to be honest with yourself and to communicate clearly with the parents. Consider your own parenting experience and how your views on discipline may have changed over time.

How do you envision your relationship with your adult children as grandparents?

a) I want to be a primary source of support and advice

b) I hope to be a fun, occasional presence in their lives

c) I want to be involved but respect their space as new parents

d) I'm open to whatever role they need me to play

This question touches on the delicate balance of supporting your adult children while respecting their autonomy as parents. Think about your current relationship with your children and how becoming a grandparent might shift those dynamics.

What's your comfort level with technology and social media in relation to your grandchildren?

a) I'm excited to connect with them through technology

b) I prefer face-to-face interactions

c) I'm willing to learn new technologies to stay connected

d) I'm comfortable with a mix of traditional and tech-based interactions

Technology can be a wonderful tool for staying connected, especially for long-distance grandparenting. Consider your current tech skills and your willingness to learn new platforms or devices to communicate with your grandchildren.

Your answers to these questions can give you insight into your natural grandparenting style. However, remember that flexibility is key. Your style may evolve over time, and you may find that you approach different situations or even different grandchildren with varying styles.

Adapting Your Style

As your grandchildren grow and family dynamics evolve, you may need to adjust your grandparenting style. Flexibility and open communication are crucial for navigating these changes. Here are some tips for staying flexible:

- **Stay open to learning:** Be willing to adapt to new parenting trends and technologies. The world of childcare is constantly evolving, and staying informed can help you support your adult children and connect with your grandchildren. This might involve reading current parenting books, attending workshops, or simply having open discussions with your children about their parenting philosophies.

- **Communicate regularly:** Check in with your adult children about what's working and what might need adjustment. Regular, open conversations can prevent misunderstandings and ensure that everyone's needs are being met. This might involve setting up monthly family meetings or having casual check ins during visits.

- **Respect developmental stages:** Your role will change as your grandchildren grow from infants to teenagers. Be prepared to adapt your approach as your grandchildren's needs and interests evolve. For example, the hands-on care you provide for an infant will be very different from the emotional support and guidance you might offer a teenager.

- **Be open to compromise:** Sometimes, you may need to blend different styles to meet the needs of multiple grandchildren or family situations. If you have grandchildren from different families, you might find that you need to adjust your approach to each family's unique dynamics and preferences.

- **Trust your instincts:** While it's important to be flexible, also trust your own wisdom and experience. You've raised children of your own, and that experience is valuable. Find a balance between being open to new ideas and trusting your own judgment.

As you embrace your new role as a grandparent, remember that there's no one "right" way to grandparent. Your journey will be as unique as your family. By managing your emotions, setting clear expectations, and finding a grandparenting style that works for you, you're laying the foundation for a rewarding and joyful grandparenting experience.

Embrace this new chapter with open arms and an open heart. The adventure of grandparenthood is just beginning, and it promises to be one of the most fulfilling roles of your life. As you navigate the challenges and celebrate the joys, remember the words of child development expert T. Berry Brazelton: "Grandparents are both teacher and role model, anchors for the younger generation and valued keepers of family history."

Your grandchildren are lucky to have you, and as you'll soon discover, you're even luckier to have them. Welcome to the wonderful world of grandparenting! This journey will be filled with love, laughter, learning, and countless precious moments. Embrace each day with enthusiasm, patience, and an open mind, and you'll find that being a grandparent is one of life's greatest gifts.

Chapter 2:
Building a Strong Relationship with Your Grandchild

The journey of grandparenthood is a remarkable one, filled with opportunities to form deep, lasting connections with the newest members of your family. This chapter explores the art of building and nurturing these precious relationships, focusing on three key aspects: establishing a strong foundation, creating unforgettable moments, and embracing the power of play. Through these avenues, you'll discover how to forge bonds that will enrich both your life and the lives of your grandchildren for years to come.

Building a Strong Relationship with Your Grandchild

The cornerstone of a meaningful relationship with your grandchild is understanding and adapting to their developmental stages. From the moment they enter the world to their journey through adolescence, your grandchild will undergo remarkable changes in their physical, cognitive, and emotional capabilities. By aligning your approach with these stages, you can create a connection that grows and evolves alongside your grandchild.

In the earliest months of life, your newborn grandchild is primarily focused on their immediate needs and is just beginning to recognize familiar faces and voices. This period, from birth to about three months, is crucial for establishing a sense of trust and security. As a grandparent, you can contribute to this foundational stage by:

- Holding your grandchild close allows them to become familiar with your scent and the sound of your heartbeat. This physical closeness mimics the comfort they experienced in the womb and helps them feel safe in your presence.

- Speaking softly and making eye contact, even if they can't yet respond. Your gentle voice and smiling face will become a source of comfort and recognition for them.

- Singing lullabies or soft songs not only soothes them but also introduces them to the rhythms and melodies of language. Don't worry about having a perfect voice – your grandchild will love the sound simply because it's you.

As Sarah, a grandmother from Ohio, shared, "I made it a point to visit my daughter and new grandson at least once a week. I would hold him close, sing softly, and just enjoy those precious moments. Now, at two years old, he still lights up when he hears my voice. It's like we have a special language all our own" (Robinson, 2023).

As your grandchild moves into the 3 to 6-month range, they become more interactive and responsive to facial expressions and tones of voice. This stage offers new opportunities for engagement:

- Introduce simple games like peek-a-boo, which not only bring joy but also help develop their understanding of object permanence – the concept that things continue to exist even when they can't be seen.

- Offer age-appropriate toys with different textures and sounds. This sensory exploration is crucial for their cognitive development and can be a fun way to interact with them.

- Begin reading simple board books, pointing out pictures, and using animated voices. Even if they don't understand the words yet, this early exposure to books can foster a lifelong love of reading.

From 6 to 12 months, your grandchild's increasing mobility and curiosity about their environment opens up even more possibilities for connection:

- Engage in floor play, encouraging crawling and exploration. This physical activity is not only fun but also crucial for their developing motor skills.

- Play simple hand games like "Pat-a-Cake" or "This Little Piggy." These games combine physical touch, rhythm, and language in a way that's engaging and developmentally appropriate.

- Introduce simple words and phrases, repeating them often. This repetition is key to language acquisition and helps your grandchild associate you with learning and discovery.

As your grandchild grows beyond the first year, your interactions will naturally evolve. Toddlers (1-3 years) thrive on activities that encourage language development and physical coordination. Reading stories with exaggerated voices, singing action songs, and engaging in simple pretend play can all be wonderful bonding experiences. Preschoolers (3-5 years) are entering a world of imagination and creativity. This is a perfect time to introduce simple crafts, engage in more complex pretend play, and begin sharing family stories and traditions. Your role as a keeper of family history becomes increasingly important at this stage.

School-age children (6-12 years) are developing their own interests and personalities. Engaging in their hobbies, playing more complex games, and having deeper conversations about their thoughts and feelings can strengthen your bond. This is also an excellent time to introduce them to your own interests and skills, creating shared experiences that can last a lifetime.

Adolescents (13+ years) may seem more challenging to connect with, but this stage offers unique opportunities for deeper relationships. As Grandfather John notes, "When my granddaughter hit her teens, I worried we'd grow apart. But by showing interest in her hobbies and offering a listening ear without judgment, we've actually grown closer. I've learned so much about her world, and I think she's gained a new perspective on mine too" (GrandkidsMatter, 2017).

Throughout all these stages, consistency and presence are key. Regular interactions, even if they're brief, help build a sense of security and anticipation in your relationship. For long-distance grandparents, technology can be a valuable tool. Video calls, text messages, and even old-fashioned letters can help maintain that crucial connection. Remember, building a strong relationship is not about grand gestures or expensive gifts. It's about being present, showing genuine interest in your grandchild's world, and creating a safe space for them to be themselves. Your unconditional love and acceptance can be a powerful force in their life, providing a sense of stability and support as they navigate the challenges of growing up.

Creating Memorable Moments

While regular interactions form the foundation of your relationship with your grandchild, creating special traditions and rituals can forge lasting memories that will be treasured for years to come. These traditions don't need to be elaborate or expensive; often, the simplest activities become the most cherished. The power of these moments lies in their ability to create a sense of continuity, belonging, and shared history between you and your grandchildren.

Annual "Grandparent Camp": Set aside a weekend each year for your grandchildren to stay with you. This dedicated time allows for deeper connections and creates anticipation throughout the year. The beauty of this tradition is its flexibility and the opportunity for creativity it provides.

When planning your "Grandparent Camp," consider choosing a theme for each year. For example, you might have a "Space Explorers" theme one year, where activities could include building model rockets, stargazing, and learning about constellations. The next year could be "Junior Chefs," focusing on cooking skills, trying new recipes, and perhaps even staging a mini cooking competition.

The key to a successful "Grandparent Camp" is in the planning and execution. Start by sending out "invitations" to your grandchildren a few months in advance. This builds excitement and gives them something to look forward to. Create a loose schedule of activities, but also allow for plenty of free time and spontaneity.

Consider including both indoor and outdoor activities to cater to different interests and weather conditions. For example, you might plan a nature scavenger hunt, followed by indoor craft time using the items collected. End each day with a special ritual, like roasting marshmallows and telling stories around a backyard fire pit. Remember, the goal isn't to create a packed itinerary but to provide opportunities for bonding and memory-making. Some of the most precious moments often happen during the unstructured times between planned activities.

Birthday Breakfasts: Start a tradition of taking each grandchild out for a special birthday breakfast, during which they can choose the restaurant and have your undivided attention. This one-on-one time is precious, allowing for deeper conversations and creating a sense of individual importance for each grandchild.

The beauty of birthday breakfasts lies in their simplicity and the individual attention they provide. In families with multiple grandchildren, this tradition ensures that each child gets their own special time with you. It's an opportunity to focus solely on them, their interests, and their growth over the past year.

To make these breakfasts even more special, consider creating a "birthday interview" tradition. Each year, ask your grandchild a set of questions about their likes, dislikes, dreams, and thoughts. Record their answers in a special notebook. Over time, this becomes a beautiful record of their growth and changing perspectives.

You might also use this time to give them a small, meaningful gift. Perhaps a book you think they'd enjoy or something related to a hobby or interest they've developed over the past year. The gift itself doesn't need to be expensive; it's the thought and personalization that counts.

Holiday Crafts: Create annual holiday-themed crafts together. For example, make ornaments each Christmas or carve pumpkins each Halloween. These crafts not only result in cherished keepsakes but also provide an opportunity to talk about family history and traditions associated with each holiday. The act of creating something together is a powerful bonding experience. It allows for conversation, creativity, and the passing down of skills. When planning holiday crafts, consider projects that can be built upon year after year. For instance, you might start a tradition of creating a new ornament each Christmas that represents something significant from that year. Over time, your grandchild's tree will be filled with memories of their life and your relationship.

Don't limit yourself to major holidays. Consider creating crafts for lesser-celebrated days, too, like making kites for the first day of spring or creating pressed flower bookmarks for the start of summer vacation. The regularity of these craft sessions creates a rhythm to your relationship and gives your grandchildren something to look forward to throughout the year.

Story Time Rituals: Establish a special reading time when you're together, complete with cozy blankets and favorite snacks. You might create a "Grandparent's Choice" book club, where you introduce them to beloved books from your childhood or let them choose new adventures to explore together.

Reading together is not just about the stories; it's about the atmosphere you create and the discussions that follow. Consider creating a special "reading nook" in your home, perhaps with a comfortable chair big enough for cuddling, good lighting, and a basket of books. You might even have special "reading blankets" that only come out during story time.

To make this tradition even more engaging, consider alternating between reading books and telling family stories. Share tales from your childhood, stories about their parents when they were young, or legends passed down through your family. This not only entertains but also helps your grandchildren understand their place in the family's larger story.

For older grandchildren, you might start a two-person book club. Choose a book to read separately, then come together to discuss it. This can lead to rich conversations about characters, plot, and life lessons, helping to deepen your connection and understanding of each other.

Nature Walks: Regular nature walks can become a cherished tradition, especially if you incorporate activities like bird watching or collecting interesting leaves or rocks. These walks provide an opportunity to teach about the natural world, engage in gentle exercise, and have uninterrupted conversations away from screens and other distractions.

The beauty of nature walks is that they can be adapted to any location and any season. In spring, you might focus on identifying wildflowers or watching for returning migratory birds. Summer could be about observing insects or identifying different types of trees. Fall lends itself to collecting colorful leaves and acorns, while winter walks might involve looking for animal tracks in the snow.

Consider creating a nature journal with your grandchild. After each walk, you can write down or draw what you observed. Over time, this becomes a beautiful record of your shared experiences and the changing seasons. You might also use these walks as an opportunity to teach about conservation and the importance of caring for the environment.

For grandparents who live far from their grandchildren, you could establish a "parallel walk" tradition. Agree to go for a nature walk at the same time, even though you're in different locations. Afterward, share photos or video calls to discuss what you each observed. This creates a sense of shared experience despite the distance.

Cooking Together: Teach your grandchildren family recipes or explore new cuisines together. This not only creates memories but also passes down cultural heritage and practical life skills. Grandmother Maria shares, "Every summer, I spend a week teaching my grandkids to make traditional Italian dishes. It's become something they look forward to all year, and it's a wonderful way to share our family history. Plus, seeing their pride when they master a recipe is priceless" (Davis, 2017).

Cooking together is a multi-sensory experience that engages all aspects of learning. It teaches math skills through measuring, science through the chemical reactions of cooking, and history through the origins of recipes. It also provides ample opportunity for conversation and the sharing of family stories.

Consider creating a special cookbook with your grandchildren. Each time you cook together, add the recipe along with notes about where it came from, any modifications you made, and memories associated with the dish. Include photos of your cooking sessions and the finished products. This becomes a treasured keepsake that your grandchildren can take with them when they start their own households.

For long-distance grandparents, consider having virtual cooking sessions. Send your grandchild a recipe and ingredients list in advance, then cook the same dish together over a video call. This can be a fun way to stay connected and share a common experience despite the distance.

When creating traditions, keep in mind:

Consistency is key. Regular rituals, even simple ones, help build anticipation and comfort. The predictability of these traditions can be especially comforting for children as they navigate the many changes of growing up. However, consistency doesn't mean rigidity. The essence of the tradition should remain constant, but the details can evolve as your grandchildren grow. Be flexible. As your grandchildren grow, be open to adapting traditions to suit their changing interests and capabilities. What worked for a five-year-old might need tweaking for a teenager, but the core of the tradition can remain. For example, your annual "Grandparent Camp" might evolve from simple crafts and games to more complex projects or even community service activities as your grandchildren mature.

Involve your grandchildren in planning. Letting them contribute ideas increases their engagement and excitement. This collaborative approach also teaches them about the effort that goes into maintaining family traditions. As they get older, give them more responsibility in planning and executing traditions. This not only keeps them engaged but also teaches valuable life skills.

Document the memories. Take photos, keep a journal, or create scrapbooks to preserve these special moments. These mementos can become treasured keepsakes and spark joy and nostalgia in years to come. Consider creating a shared online photo album where both you and your grandchildren can add photos and comments. This becomes a living record of your relationship that can be enjoyed even when you're apart.

As Finn (2022) notes, "Family traditions create a sense of belonging and identity. They give children roots, helping them feel secure in an ever-changing world." In a fast-paced society where change is constant, the stability and predictability of family traditions can be a powerful anchor for children.

Remember, the most meaningful traditions often grow organically from shared interests or spontaneous moments of joy. Pay attention to what lights up your grandchild's face or what activities they always want to repeat. These can be the seeds of traditions that will last a lifetime. Ultimately, the value of these traditions lies not in their elaborateness or cost but in the love, attention, and consistency they represent. They are tangible expressions of your commitment to your relationship with your grandchildren. Through these shared experiences, you're not just creating memories; you're weaving the fabric of your family's unique story, one precious moment at a time.

The Importance of Playtime

Play is not just about having fun; it's a crucial component of child development and an excellent way to bond with your grandchildren. Through play, children learn about the world around them, develop problem-solving skills, and build social and emotional intelligence. As a grandparent, engaging in play with your grandchild offers a unique opportunity to support their growth while strengthening your relationship.

The significance of play in a child's development cannot be overstated. It's through play that children first begin to make sense of the world around them, test boundaries, and develop crucial life skills. Play allows children to experiment with different roles, scenarios, and outcomes in a safe environment. It's their way of processing information, expressing emotions, and learning to interact with others.

For grandparents, playtime offers a wonderful opportunity to connect with grandchildren on their level. It's a chance to step out of the adult world and into the magical realm of childhood imagination. This shared experience can create lasting bonds and memories that both you and your grandchildren will treasure for years to come.

Understanding the role of play at different ages can help you engage more effectively with your grandchildren:

For infants (0-12 months), sensory play is crucial. At this stage, babies are learning about the world primarily through their senses. Offer toys with different textures, colors, and sounds to stimulate their developing senses. Soft toys, rattles, and board books are excellent choices. As you play, narrate what you're doing - this helps with language development even though they can't speak yet.

Simple games like peek-a-boo help develop object permanence - the understanding that objects continue to exist even when they can't be seen. This might seem trivial to adults, but it's a significant cognitive milestone for babies. When playing peek-a-boo, vary your facial expressions and the tone of your voice to keep the game engaging and help your grandchild learn to read emotions.

Singing and movement games support language and motor skill development. Songs with actions like "The Itsy Bitsy Spider" or "Head, Shoulders, Knees, and Toes" are not only fun but help babies start to connect words with body parts and movements. Don't worry if you're not a great singer - your grandchild will love your voice simply because it's yours.

At this stage, your animated facial expressions and gentle touch during play are as important as any toy. Babies are naturally drawn to human faces, so simply sitting with your grandchild and making different expressions can be a form of play. Gentle tickles, soft strokes, and baby massage can also be playful ways to bond and support their sensory development.

Toddlers (1-3 years) thrive on imaginative play. This is the age when children's imaginations start to flourish, and they begin to engage in pretend play. Encourage their budding creativity with dolls, stuffed animals, or toy kitchens. You might find yourself invited to tea parties with stuffed animal guests or asked to be a patient in their pretend doctor's office. When engaging in imaginative play with toddlers, follow their lead. If they hand you a banana and tell you it's a telephone, go along with it! This type of play helps develop their creativity and problem-solving skills. It also teaches them about different roles and scenarios they might encounter in real life. This is also a great time to introduce simple puzzles and shape sorters to develop problem-solving skills. Start with puzzles that have large, easy-to-grasp pieces and clear, simple images. As they master these, they gradually introduce more complex puzzles. Remember to offer praise for their efforts, not just their successes. This helps build their confidence and resilience.

Active play like gentle chasing games or dancing supports their physical development and helps burn off their abundant energy. Toddlers are constantly on the move as they explore their growing physical abilities. Games like "Simon Says" or "Follow the Leader" can be fun ways to encourage movement while also teaching listening skills and body awareness.

Preschoolers (3-5 years) are ready for more structured play. Their growing cognitive abilities and longer attention spans allow for more complex activities. Simple board games teach turn-taking and following rules, important social skills they'll need as they enter school. Games like Candy Land or Chutes and Ladders are great starter board games. As you play, model good sportsmanship - show them that it's okay to lose and how to win graciously.

Arts and crafts projects foster creativity and fine motor skills. Activities like coloring, cutting with safety scissors, or stringing large beads can help develop the fine motor skills they'll need for writing. Don't focus on creating perfect art - the process is more important than the product at this age.

Outdoor play, like riding tricycles or playing catch, supports gross motor development and provides an opportunity to teach about safety and spatial awareness. As you engage in these activities, you can naturally introduce concepts like "stop," "go," "near," and "far." This is also a great time to start teaching basic safety rules, like looking both ways before crossing a street. School-age children (6-12 years) enjoy more complex games that challenge their growing cognitive abilities. Strategy board games or card games develop critical thinking skills. Games like checkers, chess, or Uno can provide hours of entertainment while also teaching strategic thinking and planning ahead.

Building sets (like LEGO) encourage spatial awareness and problem-solving. These types of toys also allow for open-ended play, where children can let their imaginations run wild. You might find yourself helping to construct elaborate cities or spaceships! This is also a great age to introduce them to sports or other physical activities that they enjoy, creating shared interests that can last into adulthood. Whether it's playing catch in the backyard, going for bike rides, or learning a new sport together, these activities can become cherished bonding experiences.

Teenagers (13+ years) might seem less interested in traditional "play," but finding shared activities is still important. The key is to find ways to connect that respect their growing independence and changing interests.

Video games (in moderation) can be a way to connect and enjoy shared interests. While it's important to monitor screen time, playing video games together can be a fun way to bond. Many games now involve problem-solving, strategic thinking, and even physical activity (in the case of motion-controlled games).

Puzzle-solving activities or escape room games challenge their cognitive skills and provide opportunities for teamwork. These types of activities can be a great way to work together and celebrate shared accomplishments. Shared hobbies like photography, cooking, or gardening can become bonding experiences that bridge the generational gap.

These activities allow you to share your knowledge and skills while also learning from your grandchild's perspective and abilities.

When engaging in play with your grandchildren, remember:

Follow their lead. Let them guide the play and show you what interests them. This child-led approach helps build their confidence and allows them to see the world through their eyes. It also shows them that you value their ideas and choices.

Be present. Put away distractions like phones and give them your full attention. This undivided attention is a precious gift in our often-distracted world. It shows your grandchild that they are important and worthy of your full focus.

Make it educational but fun. Incorporate learning opportunities naturally into play. For example, counting pieces in a game or discussing the colors you're using in a drawing can introduce educational concepts without feeling like a lesson. The key is to keep it light and fun - if it feels like work, it's no longer play.

Be patient. Some children may take time to warm up, especially if you don't see them often. Don't force interaction; instead, create a welcoming environment where they feel comfortable joining in when they're ready. Sometimes, simply being in the same room, engaged in parallel play, can be a comfortable way to start.

Grandfather Tom shares, "I used to worry about keeping up with my energetic grandkids. But I've found that even simple activities like building block towers or reading stories together can be incredibly bonding. It's not about being the most active playmate; it's about being present and engaged. Sometimes, just sitting quietly and working on a puzzle together leads to the most wonderful conversations" (Mrs Shepherd, Doncaster, 2024).

Tom's experience highlights an important point - play doesn't always have to be high-energy or elaborate to be meaningful. Sometimes, the quieter moments of shared activity can lead to the deepest connections.

As your grandchildren grow older, the nature of your play will evolve, but its importance doesn't diminish. For older children and teenagers, "play" might take the form of shared hobbies, sports, or even intellectual discussions. The key is to find activities that you both enjoy and that allow for meaningful interaction.

Remember, play is not just about the activity itself but about the connection it fosters. It's a time for laughter, for learning about each other, and for creating memories that will last a lifetime. Through play, you're not just a grandparent but a friend, a teacher, and a trusted confidant.

Play also offers opportunities for teaching important life lessons in a natural, non-threatening way. Through games, children learn about fairness, following rules, and how to handle both winning and losing gracefully. In imaginative play, they can explore different roles and scenarios, developing empathy and social skills. Even simple activities like building with blocks can teach persistence and problem-solving.

As a grandparent, you bring a unique perspective to playtime. You have a lifetime of experiences to draw from, and you're often able to bring a sense of calm and patience that busy parents might struggle to maintain. Your play sessions can be a special time when your grandchildren feel fully seen and appreciated for who they are.

Chapter 3:
Getting around the latest parenting trends

In today's rapidly evolving world, staying informed about modern parenting practices is crucial for grandparents who want to support and relate to their adult children effectively. This chapter will explore the latest trends in parenting, focusing on technology, health and safety guidelines, and contemporary parenting philosophies.

The Role of Technology in Modern Parenting

As we venture deeper into the 21st century, technology has become an integral part of parenting, transforming the way parents raise their children and how grandparents interact with their grandchildren. From smartphone apps that meticulously track feeding schedules to social media platforms that serve as digital baby books, today's parents are navigating a digital landscape that was unimaginable just a few decades ago.

Digital Parenting Tools and Applications

One of the most significant changes in modern parenting is the proliferation of digital tools and applications designed to assist parents in their day-to-day responsibilities. These tools range from high-tech baby monitors with video capabilities to sophisticated apps that track developmental milestones with precision.

For instance, many new parents rely heavily on apps to log their baby's feeding times, diaper changes, and sleep patterns. These digital logs not only help parents stay organized in the sleep-deprived haze of early parenthood but also provide valuable data that can be shared with pediatricians during check-ups. As Dumisani Nomagugu Nkala (2024) points out, "Technology has become an indispensable tool in modern parenting, offering solutions to age-old challenges and introducing new ways to monitor and support child development" (Nkala, 2024).

Some popular parenting apps that have gained traction include:

- **Baby Tracker:** This comprehensive app allows parents to log feedings, diaper changes, and sleep patterns. It also offers features like growth tracking and photo journals, creating a complete digital record of a child's early years.

- **Wonder Weeks:** Based on scientific research, this app helps parents understand their baby's developmental leaps. It provides insights into why a baby might be fussy or clingy during certain periods and offers suggestions for activities to support their development.

- **Kinedu:** This innovative app provides personalized activities to support a child's development based on their age and stage. It offers video demonstrations of activities and tracks a child's progress across various developmental domains.

While these tools can be incredibly helpful, it's important to remember that they shouldn't replace human intuition and connection. As a grandparent, you can offer a valuable perspective on balancing technology use with hands-on parenting. Your experience in raising children without these digital aids can provide a grounding influence, reminding your adult children to trust their instincts and not become overly reliant on technology.

Social Media and Parenting

Social media has revolutionized how parents share information about their children and seek advice from others. Platforms like Facebook, Instagram, and Pinterest have become go-to resources for parenting tips, product recommendations, and community support. Many parents use these platforms to document their child's milestones, seek advice on parenting challenges, and connect with other parents facing similar experiences.

However, this constant connectivity can also lead to information overload and increased parental anxiety. As Kelsey Borresen (2024) notes, "The pressure to present a perfect image of family life online can be stressful and unrealistic for many parents" (Borresen, 2024). Many parents feel compelled to showcase only the highlight reel of their parenting journey, leading to feelings of inadequacy when comparing their reality to the curated images they see online.

Moreover, the abundance of parenting advice available on social media can be overwhelming and sometimes contradictory. Parents may find themselves inundated with conflicting information on topics ranging from sleep training to introducing solid foods, leading to confusion and self-doubt.

As a grandparent, you can provide a grounding influence by reminding your adult children that social media doesn't tell the whole story of parenting. Encourage them to trust their instincts and seek advice from trusted sources, including you, rather than relying solely on online forums or social media influencers. Your years of experience in raising children can offer a valuable perspective that cuts through the noise of online parenting debates.

Staying Connected as a Grandparent

While technology can sometimes feel overwhelming, it also offers wonderful opportunities for grandparents to stay connected with their grandchildren, especially when distance is a factor. Video calling platforms like Skype, FaceTime, or Zoom allow for face-to-face interactions, even when you can't be there in person.

Consider setting up regular video call dates with your grandchildren. You can read them stories, sing songs, or even play simple games together. For instance, you might:

- Host a virtual storytime, where you read a favorite children's book aloud.

- Play simple games like "I Spy" or "Simon Says" over video chat.

- Have a virtual dance party where you and your grandchildren can show off your moves.

- Cook together virtually, with you guiding your grandchildren through a simple recipe.

These digital interactions not only help you maintain a strong bond with your grandchildren but also support your adult children by providing them with a bit of respite. As Michaela Tučková (2024) suggests, "Technology can be a powerful tool for grandparents to maintain meaningful connections with their grandchildren, bridging physical distances and generational gaps" (Tučková, 2024).

However, it's crucial to remember that while technology can enhance your relationship with your grandchildren, it shouldn't replace in-person interactions when possible. Physical presence, hugs, and shared experiences are invaluable in building strong familial bonds. As Kate Garlinge (2024) emphasizes, "The warmth of a grandparent's hug and the joy of shared physical experiences cannot be fully replicated through digital means" (Garlinge, 2024).

Balancing Technology and Traditional Parenting

As a grandparent, you have a unique opportunity to help your adult children find a balance between leveraging technology and maintaining traditional parenting practices. Here are some ways you can support this balance:

- **Share your experiences:** Remind your adult children of the parenting challenges you faced without technology and how you overcame them. This can help put their tech-aided parenting in perspective.

- **Encourage unplugged time:** Suggest activities that don't involve screens, like outdoor play or board games, when you're with your grandchildren.

- **Be open to learning:** Show interest in the parenting apps and technologies your adult children use. This can open up conversations about their parenting choices and challenges.

- **Offer tech-free support:** Provide hands-on help with childcare when possible, giving your adult children a break from both parenting and technology.

- **Model balanced technology use:** When you're with your grandchildren, demonstrate how to use technology in moderation, balancing it with other activities and face-to-face interactions.

The role of technology in modern parenting is complex and multifaceted. While digital tools and social media platforms offer unprecedented support and information to new parents, they also present challenges in terms of information overload and pressure to present a perfect image online. As a grandparent, your role in this digital age is crucial. You can provide a link to traditional parenting wisdom while also embracing the benefits that technology offers in staying connected with your grandchildren. By offering a balanced perspective and supporting your adult children in navigating this digital parenting landscape, you can help ensure that technology enhances, rather than replaces, the human connection at the heart of parenting and grandparenting.

Remember, as SHEILA PERKINS (2024) wisely states, "Every generation has new parenting ideas, but as grandparents, our role is to support, not to judge" (PERKINS, 2024). By embracing this mindset, you can be a valuable ally to your adult children as they navigate the challenges of parenting in the digital age.

Updates on Health and Safety Guidelines

Parenting guidelines, especially those related to health and safety, have evolved significantly over the years. As a grandparent, it's essential to be aware of these changes to ensure you're providing the safest and most up-to-date care for your grandchildren. Let's delve into some of the most crucial areas where guidelines have seen substantial updates.

Nutrition Guidelines

Nutritional recommendations for infants and young children have undergone considerable changes in recent years. The American Academy of Pediatrics (AAP) now recommends exclusive breastfeeding for the first six months of life, followed by continued breastfeeding along with appropriate complementary foods for at least one year. This shift in focus towards breastfeeding is based on extensive research showing the numerous benefits of breast milk for infant health and development.

If you raised your children in an era when formula feeding was more common, this shift might surprise you. However, it's important to understand that this recommendation is not meant to shame parents who choose or need to use formula. As a grandparent, your role is to support your adult children's feeding choices, whether they choose to breastfeed, formula feed, or use a combination of both.

When it comes to introducing solid foods, current guidelines suggest waiting until around six months of age rather than the four months that were often recommended in the past. This change is based on research indicating that waiting until six months can reduce the risk of food allergies and ensure that the baby's digestive system is more developed.

Additionally, there's less emphasis now on introducing foods in a specific order. Instead, the focus is on offering a variety of nutrient-dense foods. This approach aims to expose babies to a wide range of flavors and textures, potentially reducing picky eating behaviors later in childhood. As Lund (2017) notes, "A healthy child gets ample nutrition through a varied diet, which sets the foundation for lifelong eating habits" (Lund, 2017).

Sleep Safety

Sleep safety is another area where guidelines have changed dramatically. The "Back to Sleep" campaign, launched in the 1990s, has significantly reduced the incidence of Sudden Infant Death Syndrome (SIDS). This campaign, now known as "Safe to Sleep," emphasizes the importance of placing babies on their backs to sleep.

Current sleep safety recommendations include:

- Always place babies on their backs to sleep for every sleep time, including naps.

- Use a firm sleep surface, such as a mattress in a safety-approved crib, covered by a fitted sheet.

- Keeping soft objects, toys, crib bumpers, and loose bedding out of the baby's sleep area.

- Room-sharing without bed-sharing for at least the first six months and, ideally, for the first year of life.

These guidelines might differ significantly from what you practiced when raising your own children. For instance, you might have been advised to place babies on their stomachs to sleep, or you might have used crib bumpers or soft blankets in the crib. It's crucial to follow these new recommendations when caring for your grandchildren, even if they seem counterintuitive based on your past experiences.

As Landsem and Cheetham (2022) point out, "Infant sleep practices have undergone significant changes in recent decades, driven by research on SIDS prevention. It's crucial for all caregivers, including grandparents, to stay informed about these evidence-based guidelines" (Landsem & Cheetham, 2022).

Car Seat Safety

Car seat guidelines have also evolved considerably over the years. Current recommendations suggest keeping children in rear-facing car seats until they reach the highest weight or height allowed by the seat's manufacturer. This often means keeping children rear-facing well into their second year of life or beyond, which is a significant change from past practices.

The reasoning behind this recommendation is based on crash dynamics and child physiology. Rear-facing seats provide better protection for a young child's head, neck, and spine in the event of a collision. As children grow and their bodies develop, they can transition to forward-facing seats with harnesses and eventually to booster seats.

Once children outgrow rear-facing seats, they should use a forward-facing car seat with a harness for as long as possible. After outgrowing the forward-facing seat, children should use a booster seat until they can properly fit in a vehicle seat belt. This typically occurs when they reach a height of 4 feet 9 inches and are between 8 and 12 years old.

It's worth noting that these guidelines are minimums, and many safety experts recommend extending each stage as long as possible within the limits of the car seat. As a grandparent, it's crucial to familiarize yourself with the current car seat being used for your grandchild and to follow the parents' instructions regarding its use.

Staying Updated on Guidelines

Keeping up with changing health and safety guidelines can feel overwhelming, but there are several strategies you can use to stay informed:

- **Follow reputable organizations on social media:** Organizations such as the American Academy of Pediatrics (AAP) or the Centers for Disease Control and Prevention (CDC) regularly post updates on their social media channels. Following these accounts can provide you with easy access to the latest guidelines and recommendations.

- **Subscribe to newsletters:** Many trusted parenting websites and health organizations offer newsletters that provide regular updates on child health and safety. Subscribing to these can help you stay informed about new guidelines as they're released.

- **Attend grandparenting classes:** Many local hospitals and community centers offer classes specifically designed for grandparents. These classes often cover the latest health and safety guidelines and can be an excellent way to refresh your knowledge.

- **Use reliable online resources:** Websites like HealthyChildren.org (run by the AAP) provide up-to-date, evidence-based information on a wide range of child health and safety topics.

- **Maintain open communication:** Perhaps most importantly, maintain open communication with your adult children about their parenting choices and the guidelines they follow. They are likely to be up-to-date on the latest recommendations and can guide you on how they prefer things to be done with their children.

Remember, as Writer (2019) suggests, "While grandparents bring valuable experience to childcare, it's crucial to stay open to new, evidence-based practices that may differ from what was common in previous generations" (Writer, 2019).

As a grandparent, your role in supporting your grandchildren's health and safety is invaluable. By staying informed about current guidelines and working in partnership with your adult children, you can provide the safest and most nurturing care possible for your grandchildren.

It's natural to feel some resistance to changes in practices that you've long considered safe and effective. However, it's important to remember that these new guidelines are based on extensive research and are designed to provide the best possible outcomes for children.

Your willingness to adapt and learn new practices demonstrates your commitment to your grandchildren's well-being and sets a powerful example of lifelong learning.

Contemporary Parenting Philosophies

Today's parents have access to a wide range of parenting philosophies, each with its own set of principles and practices. As a grandparent, understanding these approaches can help you better support your adult children's parenting decisions. Let's explore some of the most popular contemporary parenting philosophies in detail.

Attachment Parenting

Attachment parenting, popularized by Dr. William Sears in the 1980s, emphasizes the importance of a strong emotional bond between parent and child. This philosophy is rooted in attachment theory, which suggests that a secure attachment in infancy leads to better emotional and social development later in life.

The key principles of attachment parenting include:

- **Responding promptly to the baby's cries:** Attachment parenting advocates believe that quick responses to a baby's cries help build trust and security. This doesn't mean that parents should rush to pick up the baby at every sound, but rather that they should be attentive and responsive to their baby's needs.

- **Babywearing:** This involves carrying the baby in a sling or carrier, keeping them close to the parent's body. Proponents argue that this practice promotes bonding, allows the baby to observe and learn from the parent's activities, and can be calming for fussy babies.

- **Co-sleeping or room-sharing:** Attachment parenting encourages keeping the baby close during sleep times. This can range from having the baby sleep in the same room as the parents to having the baby sleep in the same bed (although many pediatricians caution against bed-sharing due to safety concerns).

- **Extended breastfeeding:** While recognizing that not all mothers can or choose to breastfeed, attachment parenting encourages breastfeeding beyond infancy, often until the child self-weans.

- **Positive discipline:** This involves using gentle guidance and redirection rather than punishment to teach children appropriate behavior.

If your adult children practice attachment parenting, you might notice they're more likely to keep their baby close and respond quickly to their cries rather than letting the baby "cry it out." They may also be more likely to continue breastfeeding into toddlerhood and beyond.

As Kate Garlinge (2024) notes, "Attachment parenting is about creating a strong, secure bond with your child from the earliest days. This foundation of trust and security is believed to foster confidence and independence as the child grows" (Garlinge, 2024).

Montessori Parenting

Inspired by the educational philosophy of Maria Montessori, this approach focuses on fostering independence and natural development in children. Montessori parenting extends the principles of Montessori education into the home environment.

Key aspects of Montessori parenting include:

- **Providing a prepared environment:** This involves creating spaces in the home that allow for exploration and learning. A Montessori-inspired home often features low shelves with carefully selected toys, child-sized furniture, and areas set up for independent play and learning.

- **Encouraging child-led activities:** Montessori parenting emphasizes following the child's interests and allowing them to choose their activities. This approach believes that children are naturally motivated to learn and explore when given the right environment and freedom.

- **Using natural materials and real-world tools:** Montessori favors toys and tools made from natural materials like wood, metal, and fabric over plastic. They also encourage the use of real-world tools sized for children, such as small brooms for cleaning or child-sized kitchen utensils for cooking.

- **Fostering practical life skills:** From a young age, children are encouraged to participate in household tasks and care for themselves. This might include activities like pouring their own drinks, helping with meal preparation, or learning to dress themselves.

- **Respecting the child:** Montessori parenting emphasizes treating children with respect, speaking to them calmly and clearly, and involving them in decision-making processes when appropriate.

Ebisujima (2024) explains, "Montessori parenting is about creating an environment that supports your child's natural development. It's about giving them the tools and opportunities to learn and grow at their own pace" (Ebisujima, 2024).

Positive Parenting

Positive parenting, also known as positive discipline, focuses on building a strong, deeply committed relationship between parent and child based on communication and mutual respect. This approach emphasizes guidance over punishment and seeks to understand the reasons behind a child's behavior.

Key principles of positive parenting include:

- **Setting clear expectations and limits:** Positive parenting doesn't mean being permissive. Instead, it involves setting clear, age-appropriate boundaries and consistently enforcing them.

- **Using positive reinforcement:** This approach focuses on praising good behavior rather than punishing bad behavior. The idea is to encourage children to repeat positive actions by giving them attention and approval.

- **Encouraging problem-solving skills:** Instead of solving problems for children, positive parenting encourages parents to guide children in finding their own solutions. This helps develop critical thinking and independence.

- **Fostering emotional intelligence:** Positive parenting places a strong emphasis on helping children understand and manage their emotions. This involves acknowledging and validating children's feelings, even when their behavior isn't acceptable.

- **Using natural consequences:** When children misbehave, positive parenting advocates for allowing them to experience the natural consequences of their actions (as long as it's safe to do so) rather than imposing punishments.

Parents who follow this approach might use phrases like "I understand you're feeling frustrated" instead of immediately scolding a child for misbehavior. They might also involve children in creating family rules and problem-solving when issues arise.

Michaela Tučková (2024) states, "Positive parenting is about building a relationship of trust and respect with your child. It's not always easy, but the long-term benefits in terms of your child's emotional development and your family dynamics can be significant" (Tučková, 2024).

Supporting Different Parenting Philosophies

As a grandparent, it's important to respect and support your adult children's chosen parenting philosophy, even if it differs from how you raised your own children. Here are some ways to do this:

- **Ask questions to understand their approach better:** Show genuine interest in learning about their parenting philosophy. Ask open-ended questions about why they've chosen this approach and how it works for their family.

- **Read about their chosen philosophy:** Take the initiative to educate yourself about their parenting approach. This can help you understand the reasoning behind their decisions and practices.

- **Observe how they interact with their children and follow their lead:** When you're with your grandchildren, pay attention to how your adult children handle different situations. Try to mimic their approach when you're caring for the grandchildren.

- **Offer support without judgment:** Even if you don't fully agree with their parenting style, offer your support. Remember that parenting is challenging, and your adult children need your encouragement.

- **Be willing to adapt your own behavior:** When caring for your grandchildren, be prepared to do things differently than you might have done with your own children. This might mean learning new techniques or refraining from practices you previously used.

- **Communicate openly:** If you have concerns or questions about their parenting approach, discuss these openly and respectfully. Choose an appropriate time when the children aren't present.

- **Respect their decisions:** Remember that as parents, your adult children have the final say in how they are raised. Even if you disagree, it's important to respect their choices.

Remember, your role is to support your adult children in their parenting journey, not to compete or undermine their choices. By showing respect for their decisions, you're more likely to be included in your grandchildren's lives and have opportunities to share your own wisdom and experiences.

As SHEILA PERKINS (2024) wisely states, "Every generation has new parenting ideas, but as grandparents, our role is to support, not to judge" (PERKINS, 2024). By embracing this mindset, you can be a valuable ally to your adult children as they navigate the challenges of modern parenting.

Chapter 4:
Long-Distance Grandparenting: Nurturing Connections Across Miles

In today's increasingly mobile world, many grandparents find themselves living far away from their grandchildren. This physical distance can be challenging, but it doesn't have to be a barrier to building strong, loving relationships. This chapter will explore effective strategies for nurturing a deep connection with your grandchildren, even when you're miles apart. We'll delve into the virtual ways of staying connected, creative communication methods, and how to make the most of your in-person visits.

The Virtual Way: Maximizing Digital Connections

In today's interconnected world, technology has become a powerful tool for long-distance grandparents to maintain strong, meaningful relationships with their grandchildren. Video calls, in particular, have emerged as an invaluable resource, offering face-to-face interactions that can bridge the physical gap between generations. Platforms like Skype, FaceTime, and Zoom have revolutionized the way we communicate, allowing grandparents to be present in their grandchildren's lives, even from afar.

Making the Most of Video Calls

While video calls provide a platform for visual and auditory connection, the key to truly impactful virtual visits lies in making these interactions engaging and meaningful. As Kerry (2019) aptly points out, "Regular video calls can help maintain a strong bond between grandparents and grandchildren, but the key is to make these calls interactive and fun" (Kerry, 2019). This observation underscores the importance of not just scheduling calls but also planning how to make the most of this digital time together.

One of the fundamental aspects of successful video calls is establishing a routine. Consistency in your virtual visits can help create a sense of anticipation and excitement, especially for younger grandchildren. Consider setting up a regular schedule for your calls, whether it's weekly or bi-weekly, depending on your family's availability. This regularity not only gives children something to look forward to but also helps integrate you into their routine, even from a distance.

Preparation is another crucial element in enhancing your video call experiences. Before each call, take some time to plan activities that you can do together. This forethought can transform a potentially awkward or stilted interaction into a fun, engaging experience for both you and your grandchildren. The activities you choose can vary widely depending on the age and interests of your grandchildren.

For younger children, consider having props ready to use during the call. Puppets, toys, or other objects can be excellent tools for engagement. You might create a simple puppet show, use toys to act out stories, or even incorporate everyday objects into imaginative play. These props can help capture and maintain the attention of younger children who might otherwise find it challenging to focus on a screen for extended periods.

If you have a mobile device, you can take your grandchildren on virtual tours of your home, garden, or neighborhood. This simple act can help them feel more connected to your daily life and environment. You might show them your garden and talk about the plants you're growing or take them on a walk around your neighborhood, pointing out interesting sights along the way. This not only provides visual stimulation but also helps your grandchildren feel like they're a part of your world, even from afar.

Sharing experiences is another powerful way to connect during video calls. Many video-calling platforms offer screen-sharing features, which you can use to look at photos or videos together. This could include recent pictures from your activities or old family photos that tell stories about your family history. Sharing these visual memories can spark conversations, allow you to share family stories, and help your grandchildren develop a sense of their family heritage.

It's important to remember that young children often have short attention spans, especially when it comes to digital interactions. Be prepared to be patient and flexible during your calls. If you notice your grandchild becoming restless or losing interest, be ready to switch activities or even end the call if necessary. The quality of the interaction is more important than the quantity of time spent on the call.

Interactive Activities for Virtual Visits

Engaging your grandchildren during virtual visits is crucial for maintaining their interest and strengthening your bond. The key is to make these interactions as interactive and immersive as possible, creating shared experiences despite the physical distance.

One of the most timeless ways to connect with children is through storytelling. Virtual storytime can be a wonderful way to engage with your grandchildren during video calls. When choosing books, opt for those with large, colorful illustrations that are easy to see on screen. You might even consider using digital books that allow you to share your screen, ensuring your grandchild can see the pictures clearly. For older children, you could start a virtual book club, where you both read the same book separately and then discuss it during your calls. This not only encourages reading but also provides a structured activity for your interactions.

Online games can also be a fun way to interact during video calls. There are numerous multiplayer online games suitable for different age groups. For younger children, simple games like tic-tac-toe or I Spy can be played easily over video. For older children, you might explore more complex online games that you can play together. The shared experience of playing a game can create a sense of togetherness and provide natural topics for conversation.

Virtual craft sessions are another excellent way to engage with your grandchildren. Plan simple craft projects that you can do together over video calls. The key here is preparation - send the necessary materials to your grandchildren in advance, then guide them through the project during your call. This not only provides a fun, hands-on activity but also allows you to teach and share skills with your grandchildren.

Encouraging your grandchildren to share their latest achievements, artwork, or favorite toys during the calls can be a great way to stay updated on their interests and accomplishments. This "show and tell" approach allows your grandchildren to take the lead in the conversation, sharing what's important to them. It also gives you insight into their daily lives and interests, providing talking points for future interactions. For a more active interaction, consider having virtual dance parties. Put on some music and have a dance party together. This is a great way to get everyone moving and laughing, creating a joyful, shared experience. You might even take turns choosing the music, allowing you to share your favorite songs with your grandchildren and vice versa.

For older grandchildren, cooking or baking together over video calls can be a rewarding experience. Plan simple recipes that you can make together, with each of you in your own kitchen. This not only teaches them valuable skills but also creates shared experiences and memories. You might even use family recipes, allowing you to pass down culinary traditions.

The JubileeTV Blog (2024) emphasizes the importance of these interactive activities, stating, "Engaging activities during video calls can transform these digital interactions into meaningful, memory-making experiences" (JubileeTV Blog, 2024). This underscores the idea that with a little creativity and planning, virtual visits can be just as impactful as in-person interactions.

Remember, the goal of these virtual interactions is to create shared experiences and memories, even when you can't be physically present. As Feister (2019) aptly notes, "The key to successful long-distance grandparenting is creativity and consistency" (Feister, 2019). This means not only coming up with engaging activities but also maintaining regular contact.

It's also important to be adaptable in your approach. What works for one grandchild might not work for another, and what's engaging one week might not hold their interest the next. Be prepared to try different activities and approaches, always keeping in mind the unique personalities and interests of your grandchildren.

Creative Communication: Beyond Video Calls

While video calls have become a primary means of staying connected with long-distance grandchildren, they are not the only way to nurture these precious relationships. Other forms of communication can be equally meaningful and sometimes even more impactful. In this section, we'll explore creative ways to maintain a strong connection with your grandchildren beyond the realm of real-time digital interactions.

The Power of Letters and Emails

In our fast-paced digital world, the art of letter writing may seem outdated. However, receiving a physical letter or a thoughtful email can be a special and memorable experience for children. As Karen Kimerer (2023) aptly points out, "Physical mail stands out in a world dominated by digital communication, making it a powerful tool for creating lasting impressions" (Kimerer, 2023). This observation underscores the unique impact that tangible, personalized communication can have in our increasingly digital lives.

For younger grandchildren, the excitement of receiving colorful postcards or letters adorned with stickers can be palpable. The tactile nature of physical mail - the feel of the paper, the sight of handwritten words, the excitement of opening an envelope - creates a multisensory experience that digital communication can't replicate. As they grow older, more detailed letters or emails discussing their interests, asking about their lives, and sharing their own experiences can help deepen your relationship.

One engaging idea for correspondence is to create a story together. You could start a story in one letter or email and ask your grandchild to continue it in their reply. This ongoing project not only sparks creativity but also maintains regular communication. It gives both you and your grandchild something to look forward to and can become a treasured keepsake over time.

Sharing family history through your correspondence is another powerful way to connect with your grandchildren. Use your letters or emails to share stories about your childhood or your grandchild's parent when they were young. These stories help connect your grandchild to their family heritage, giving them a sense of their roots and where they come from. You might share funny anecdotes, family traditions, or important life lessons you've learned over the years.

Responding to your grandchild's interests is crucial in maintaining engaging correspondence. If your grandchild mentions a new hobby or interest, use your next letter or email to ask more about it or share related information you've found. This shows that you're paying attention to what's important to them and are interested in their lives. It can also open up new avenues for conversation and shared interests.

For physical letters, including small surprises can add an extra element of excitement. Consider including flat items like bookmarks, pressed flowers, or interesting newspaper clippings. These little extras make the experience of receiving mail even more special and give your grandchild something tangible to keep.

When writing to younger children, using themed stationery can make letters more exciting. Stationery featuring their favorite characters or themes can make the act of receiving and reading a letter more engaging and fun.

Remember, as Hendricks (2023) suggests, "The most engaging emails are those that feel personal and relevant to the recipient" (Hendricks, 2023). This advice applies equally to physical letters. The key is to make your communication personal, showing that you've put thought and effort into connecting with your grandchild in a meaningful way.

Care Packages: Sending Love in a Box

Care packages are another wonderful way to maintain a connection with your grandchildren. These packages, tailored to your grandchild's interests and age, serve as a tangible reminder of your love and thoughtfulness. They bridge the physical distance between you, allowing you to share experiences and create moments of joy, even when you're far apart.

According to badgesforall (2019), "Care packages have a long history of boosting morale and maintaining connections across distances" (badgesforall, 2019). This observation highlights the emotional impact that receiving a carefully curated package can have. For a child, the excitement of receiving a package in the mail, especially one filled with items chosen just for them, can be a thrilling experience.

One approach to creating meaningful care packages is to base them on themes. For example, you might create a "Rainy Day Fun" package filled with indoor activities like puzzles, coloring books, or craft supplies. A "Beach Day" themed package could include sunglasses, a small beach toy, and a book about ocean life. A "Cozy Winter Night" package might contain a hot chocolate mix, fuzzy socks, and a collection of short stories to read together over a video call. These themed packages not only provide entertainment but also show that you're thinking about your grandchild's experiences and trying to enhance them, even from afar.

Holiday-specific packages are another great idea. Sending packages for various holidays throughout the year, including some small gifts and holiday-themed activities or decorations, can help you be part of your grandchild's holiday celebrations. This might include Valentine's Day cards to distribute to classmates, Easter egg decorating kits, or Halloween costume accessories.

For school-age children, educational packages can be both fun and beneficial. Consider sending books, educational games, or science experiment kits that align with what they're learning in school. This not only supports their learning but also shows your interest in their education and can provide topics for future conversations.

Comfort packages can be particularly meaningful. Sending items that provide comfort, such as a soft blanket, a stuffed animal, or a framed photo of you together, can help your grandchild feel close to you even when you're physically far apart. These items can serve as a tangible reminder of your love and presence in their life.

For older children or grandchildren who show an interest in cooking, consider sending baking or cooking kits. Include the ingredients and recipe for a simple project you can do together over a video call. This not only provides a fun activity but also allows you to share family recipes and create shared experiences.

Remember, as Gratitude (2012) emphasizes, "The personal touch in a care package can have a profound emotional impact" (Gratitude, 2012). Always include a personal note in each package explaining the items and expressing your love. This personal touch transforms the package from a simple collection of items into a heartfelt expression of your care and affection.

Making Visit Plans: Maximizing In-Person Time

While virtual connections and long-distance communication methods are valuable, nothing quite replaces the joy of in-person visits. These face-to-face interactions allow for physical affection, shared experiences, and the creation of lasting memories. However, these visits require careful planning to ensure they're enjoyable and meaningful for everyone involved.

When planning your visits, communication with the parents is key. Discuss the timing and duration of your visit well in advance. Be open to their suggestions and respectful of their schedules. Remember that while you're excited to spend time with your grandchildren, you're also entering into the family's established routines and dynamics.

It's a good idea to plan some activities in advance of your visit. Have some ideas for things you'd like to do with your grandchildren, but be flexible and open to their preferences, too. This might include outings to local attractions, cooking favorite meals together, or engaging in hobbies that you share. Having some plans can help structure your time together and ensure that you make the most of your visit.

When you're visiting, it's crucial to respect household rules and routines. Ask about any specific guidelines or schedules that the family follows, and be sure to adhere to them during your stay. This might include rules about screen time, dietary restrictions, or bedtime routines. Following these rules shows respect for the parents' decisions and helps maintain consistency for the children.

While it's natural to want to help out during your visit, be careful not to overstep. Offer assistance with childcare or household tasks, but be mindful not to take over or make the parents feel like their authority is being undermined. The goal is to support the family, not to replace or challenge the parents' roles. If you have multiple grandchildren, try to plan for some one-on-one time with each of them during your visit. This individual attention can be very special for each child and allows you to focus on their specific interests and needs.

Remember, the quality of time spent together is more important than the quantity. Make every moment count by being fully engaged and creating meaningful experiences. Put away distractions like phones or tablets when interacting with your grandchildren, giving them your full attention and presence. Lastly, be prepared for the emotional aspects of these visits. Arrivals and departures can be particularly challenging, especially for younger children. Have strategies in place for making these transitions easier, such as planning a special goodbye ritual or scheduling your next visit or video call before you leave.

Planning Enjoyable and Hassle-Free Visits

When it comes to visiting your grandchildren, especially if you live far away, careful planning is essential to ensure that your time together is enjoyable, meaningful, and stress-free for everyone involved. Let's delve deeper into the key aspects of planning successful visits.

Communicate Clearly with the Parents

The foundation of a successful visit begins with clear and open communication with your adult children - the parents of your grandchildren. It's crucial to discuss the timing and duration of your visit well in advance. This allows the parents to plan around your visit and ensures that your presence doesn't disrupt their regular routines or commitments. When discussing your visit, be open to the parents' suggestions and respectful of their schedules. Remember that while you're excited to spend time with your grandchildren, you're entering into their established family dynamics. Ask about any upcoming events or activities that might affect your visit. For instance, if the children have school commitments or extracurricular activities, you'll want to plan around these.

It's also a good idea to discuss expectations for the visit. Will you be staying in their home or nearby? Will you be expected to help with childcare or household tasks? Having these conversations upfront can prevent misunderstandings and ensure that everyone is on the same page.

Plan Activities in Advance

While spontaneity can be fun, having some activities planned in advance can help structure your time together and ensure that you make the most of your visit. Consider the ages and interests of your grandchildren when planning activities. For younger children, this might include trips to local parks or playgrounds, simple craft projects, or storytime sessions. For older children, you might plan outings to museums and sporting events or engage in shared hobbies.

However, it's important to be flexible and open to your grandchildren's preferences too. They might have ideas about what they want to do with you, or their interests might have changed since your last visit. Be prepared to adjust your plans based on their input and current interests. Also, consider the energy levels and attention spans of your grandchildren. It's often a good idea to balance more active, high-energy activities with quieter, more relaxed ones. This can help prevent overstimulation and ensure that both you and your grandchildren have time to recharge.

Respect Household Rules

Every family has its own set of rules and routines, and it's crucial that you respect and follow these during your visit. Ask about any household rules or routines before your visit. This might include rules about screen time, dietary restrictions, discipline methods, or bedtime routines.

Following these rules shows respect for the parents' decisions and helps maintain consistency for the children. It also demonstrates to your grandchildren that you and their parents are on the same team, which can strengthen family bonds and prevent confusion or conflict.

Offer Help, But Don't Take Over

While it's natural to want to help out during your visit, it's important to strike a balance between being helpful and not overstepping. Offer assistance with childcare or household tasks, but be mindful not to take over or make the parents feel like their authority is being undermined.

For example, you might offer to prepare meals, help with bedtime routines, or take the children on outings to give the parents a break. However, always check with the parents first and follow their lead. The goal is to support the family, not to replace or challenge the parents' roles.

Plan for One-on-One Time

If you have multiple grandchildren, try to plan for some one-on-one time with each of them during your visit. This individual attention can be very special for each child and allows you to focus on their specific interests and needs.

One-on-one time doesn't have to be elaborate. It could be as simple as taking a walk together, working on a puzzle, or having a special conversation over ice cream. These individual moments can help strengthen your bond with each grandchild and create lasting memories.

Honoring Parents' Routines and Boundaries

Respecting the parents' established routines and boundaries is crucial for maintaining family harmony and ensuring that your visits are welcome. As Sedgebrook (2020) advises, "Respecting the parents' rules and routines helps maintain family harmony and ensures your visits are welcome" (Sedgebrook, 2020). Let's explore some specific ways to honor these boundaries.

Stick to Established Routines

Children thrive on routine, and disrupting these routines can lead to stress and behavioral issues. During your visit, make an effort to follow the children's regular schedules for meals, naps, and bedtimes. This consistency helps the children feel secure and can make the transition back to normal routines easier after your visit.

If you're unsure about the daily schedule, don't hesitate to ask the parents. They'll likely appreciate your effort to maintain their routines. Remember, while you might be tempted to let routines slide for "special time" with grandchildren, maintaining consistency is often more beneficial in the long run.

Ask Before Giving Treats or Gifts

It's natural to want to spoil your grandchildren with treats or gifts, but it's important to check with the parents first. This helps avoid undermining their rules or dietary choices. Some families might have restrictions on sugar intake, screen time, or certain types of toys. By asking first, you show respect for the parents' decisions and avoid putting them in the awkward position of having to say no to something you've already given.

When it comes to gifts, consider experiences over material items. A special outing or activity can create lasting memories without adding clutter to the home. If you do bring gifts, try to choose items that align with the family's values and lifestyle.

Respect Parenting Decisions

Even if you disagree with certain parenting choices, it's important to respect and follow them during your visit. Parenting styles and philosophies have evolved over time, and what worked when you were raising children might not be the approach your adult children have chosen.

This might mean adapting to unfamiliar practices, such as baby-led weaning, gentle parenting techniques, or specific approaches to discipline. While it might be tempting to offer advice based on your experience, remember that your role is to support, not to criticize or undermine.

Offer Support Without Criticism

If you notice the parents are struggling with something, offer support in a non-judgmental way. This could be as simple as offering to take the children out for a while to give the parents a break or helping with household tasks to lighten their load.

If you do have concerns or suggestions, choose an appropriate time to discuss these privately with the parents, away from the children. Frame your thoughts as observations or questions rather than criticisms. For example, "I noticed Billy seems to have trouble settling down at bedtime. Is there anything I can do to help with the bedtime routine?"

Making the Most of Limited In-Person Time

When your visits are infrequent, it's important to make the most of your time together. Here are some detailed suggestions for maximizing your in-person interactions:

Be Fully Present

In our digital age, it's easy to be distracted by phones, tablets, or other devices. However, to truly connect with your grandchildren, it's crucial to be fully present during your time together. Put away your phone and other distractions to focus entirely on your grandchildren during your visit.

This doesn't mean you can't take photos or make necessary calls, but try to limit these activities. Your undivided attention is one of the greatest gifts you can give your grandchildren. It shows them that they are important and valued, and it allows you to fully engage in the moments you're sharing.

Create Traditions

Establishing special activities or outings that you do during each visit can create cherished traditions that your grandchildren look forward to. These traditions don't have to be elaborate – they could be as simple as making pancakes together on Saturday morning, having a movie night with popcorn, or going for ice cream at a specific local shop.

Traditions provide a sense of continuity and connection, even when you're apart. They give your grandchildren something to anticipate and remember, strengthening your bond across the miles and years.

Capture Memories

While it's important to be present in the moment, there's also value in capturing memories from your visits. Take photos or videos during your visit, but be sure to balance documentation with actual interaction. You might designate specific times for taking photos or involve your grandchildren in the process by letting them take some pictures, too.

Consider creating a shared digital album where you can add photos from your visits. This gives the whole family a way to revisit and share memories between visits.

Share Your Skills

Teaching your grandchildren something you're good at can be a wonderful way to connect and create lasting memories. Whether it's a hobby like knitting or gardening, a skill like baking or woodworking, or sharing a family recipe, passing on your knowledge creates a special bond.

These shared activities not only provide quality time together but also give your grandchildren a tangible connection to their family heritage. They might remember you every time they use the skill you taught them, even when you're not there.

Plan for Quiet Times, Too

While it's tempting to fill every moment with activities, it's also important to allow for some quiet, relaxed time together. These moments of downtime can often lead to meaningful conversations and connections. It might be reading books together, taking a leisurely walk, or simply sitting and chatting.

These quieter moments also give both you and your grandchildren time to recharge, preventing the overwhelm or exhaustion that can sometimes come with packed schedules.

As Gina Kemp, M.A. et al. (2023) emphasize, "The quality of time spent together is more important than the quantity. Make every moment count by being fully engaged and creating meaningful experiences" (Kemp et al., 2023). This reminder underscores the importance of focusing on creating meaningful interactions rather than trying to cram too much into your visits.

Chapter 5:
Balancing Grandparenting with Personal Life

Becoming a grandparent is undoubtedly one of life's most joyous experiences, bringing with it a renewed sense of purpose and an abundance of love. However, it also presents a unique challenge: how to balance the desire to be an involved grandparent with the need to maintain one's personal life and interests. This delicate balancing act is crucial for both the well-being of the grandparent and the overall health of the family dynamic.

The role of a grandparent in modern society has evolved significantly. As GrandkidsMatter (2024) points out, "Involved grandparenting requires a delicate balance between being present for your grandchildren and maintaining your own life and interests" (GrandkidsMatter, 2024). This observation highlights the complexity of the modern grandparenting role, where expectations of involvement are often higher than in previous generations.

The Importance of Personal Well-being and Self-care

As grandparents, it's all too easy to become so wrapped up in the needs and wants of our grandchildren that we neglect our own well-being. However, maintaining personal well-being and practicing self-care is crucial not only for our own health but also for our ability to be present and energetic grandparents.

Self-care is not selfish; it's a necessary component of being an effective and loving grandparent. As Keith Condie and Sarah Condie (2023) note, "Grandparenting is a balancing act that requires attention to both the needs of grandchildren and the personal needs of the grandparent" (Condie & Condie, 2023). This perspective underscores the importance of self-care in the grandparenting journey.

Practical Self-care Routines and Activities

Incorporating self-care into your daily routine doesn't have to be complicated or time-consuming. Here are some practical self-care activities that can help maintain your physical and emotional well-being:

- **Regular Exercise:** Engaging in physical activity not only keeps you healthy but also boosts your energy levels. This could be as simple as a daily walk, joining a yoga class, or swimming. For instance, Sarah, a grandmother of three, found that her morning yoga routine not only improved her flexibility but also gave her the energy to keep up with her active grandchildren during their weekly visits. "I used to feel exhausted after a day with the grandkids," Sarah shares. "But since I started doing yoga every morning, I've noticed I have much more stamina. I can keep up with their energy, and I even sleep better at night."

- **Mindfulness and Meditation:** Taking time for quiet reflection can help reduce stress and improve overall mental health. Apps like Headspace or Calm can guide you through simple meditation exercises. John, a grandfather of two, credits his daily 10-minute meditation practice with helping him stay patient and present during his grandchildren's often chaotic visits. "With two energetic grandsons, things can get pretty hectic," John explains. "But my daily meditation helps me stay calm and focused. I'm able to enjoy our time together more fully without getting overwhelmed."

- **Hobbies and Interests:** Maintaining your personal interests is vital. Whether it's gardening, reading, painting, or playing an instrument, these activities can provide a sense of personal fulfillment. Mary, a grandmother of four, found that her weekly painting class not only provided her with personal joy but also gave her a fun activity to share with her grandchildren. "I was worried that my painting hobby would take time away from my grandkids," Mary admits. "But it's actually brought us closer. They love coming over to paint with me, and it's become our special bonding activity."

- **Social Connections:** Maintaining relationships with friends and peers is important for emotional well-being. Regular coffee dates, book clubs, or community activities can provide valuable social interaction. Tom, a grandfather of three, found that his weekly golf game with friends provided him with much-needed adult conversation and a break from grandparenting duties. "Don't get me wrong, I love my grandkids," Tom says. "But having that time with my friends keeps me grounded. It's like recharging my batteries so I can be fully present when I'm with the little ones."

- **Healthy Eating:** A balanced diet can significantly impact your energy levels and overall health. Preparing nutritious meals for yourself sets a good example for your grandchildren and ensures you have the stamina to keep up with them. Lisa, a grandmother of two, noticed a significant difference in her grandparents after she started prioritizing her health. "After I started eating better and exercising regularly, I found I had so much more energy to play with my grandkids," she says. "I went from getting tired after an hour to being able to spend a whole day with them without feeling exhausted."

The Impact of Physical and Emotional Wellness on Grandparenting

Your physical and emotional wellness directly affects your ability to be an engaged and effective grandparent. When you're feeling healthy and balanced, you have more energy to play with your grandchildren, more patience to deal with challenging behaviors, and more creativity to come up with fun activities.

Bethesda Health Group (2023) emphasizes this point, stating, "Maintaining your own health and well-being is crucial for being an active and engaged grandparent. It allows you to fully participate in activities with your grandchildren and create lasting memories" (big-admin, 2023). This highlights the direct link between a grandparent's well-being and their ability to be present and active in their grandchildren's lives.

Moreover, taking care of your emotional well-being allows you to be more present and emotionally available for your grandchildren. When you're managing your own stress effectively, you're better equipped to handle the emotional needs of your grandchildren and to provide a calming presence in their lives.

David, a grandfather of four, shares his experience: "I used to get easily frustrated when my grandkids would act up. But since I've been focusing on my own emotional health through therapy and mindfulness practices, I find I'm much more patient. I can see beyond the behavior to what they really need, whether it's attention, reassurance, or just a hug."

The benefits of maintaining your own well-being extend beyond your interactions with your grandchildren. It also sets a positive example for them about the importance of self-care and personal health. As Lexi Dwyer (2021) points out, "By taking care of yourself, you're modeling healthy behaviors for your grandchildren. They learn from watching you prioritize your physical and mental health" (Dwyer, 2021).

Balancing Act: Strategies for Harmony

Finding the right balance between grandparenting and personal life is an ongoing process that may require some trial and error. Here are some strategies that can help:

- **Establish Clear Boundaries:** Communicate openly with your adult children about your availability and limitations. It's okay to say no sometimes or to set specific days for grandparenting duties.

- **Schedule Personal Time:** Just as you schedule time with your grandchildren, make sure to schedule time for your own activities and interests.

- **Involve Grandchildren in Your Interests:** Where appropriate, find ways to include your grandchildren in your hobbies or activities. This can create special bonding opportunities while allowing you to maintain your interests.

- **Prioritize Self-Care:** Make self-care activities non-negotiable parts of your routine. Remember, taking care of yourself enables you to be a better grandparent.

- **Stay Flexible:** While boundaries are important, also be open to adjusting your schedule when special needs or opportunities arise.

- **Communicate Regularly:** Keep open lines of communication with your adult children about your needs and theirs. Regular check-ins can help prevent misunderstandings and ensure everyone's needs are being met.

By implementing these strategies and prioritizing both your grandparenting role and your personal well-being, you can create a fulfilling and balanced life that allows you to be the best grandparent possible while also taking care of yourself.

Pursuing Hobbies and Interests

While being a grandparent is undoubtedly a significant and rewarding role, it's crucial to remember that it's not your sole identity. Maintaining your personal hobbies and interests is vital for your sense of self and overall life satisfaction. It also sets a positive example for your grandchildren about the importance of lifelong learning and personal growth.

As Stephen F. Duncan (2020) notes, "Grandparents who maintain their own interests and hobbies not only enrich their own lives but also provide valuable life lessons to their grandchildren about the importance of personal growth and lifelong learning" (Duncan, 2020). This perspective underscores the dual benefit of pursuing personal passions: it enhances the grandparent's life while also setting a positive example for the younger generation.

Balancing Grandparenting and Personal Passions

Finding a balance between grandparenting and personal interests can be challenging, but many grandparents have successfully navigated this terrain. Let's explore some real-life examples in more detail: Robert, a passionate amateur photographer, initially struggled with feelings of guilt when pursuing his hobby. He worried that every moment spent behind the camera was a moment he could have been spending with his grandchildren. However, Robert found an innovative way to integrate his passion into his grandparenting role. He now organizes regular "photo safaris" with his grandchildren in local parks and nature reserves.

"At first, I thought I had to choose between my photography and spending time with my grandkids," Robert shares. "But then I realized I could combine the two. Now, our photo safaris are something we all look forward to. The kids are learning about composition, light, and patience, and I'm getting to share my passion with them. It's created a special bond between us."

Robert's experience highlights how personal interests can be woven into grandparenting activities, creating unique and meaningful experiences for both generations.

Linda, an avid traveler, initially feared that becoming a grandmother would significantly curtail her adventures. She worried that the responsibilities of grandparenthood would tie her to one place, limiting her ability to explore the world. However, Linda found a creative solution that allowed her to continue her travels while also strengthening her relationships with her grandchildren.

"I've always believed that travel broadens the mind," Linda explains. "So, I started planning annual trips with each of my grandchildren once they reached a certain age. It's become a rite of passage in our family. Not only do I get to indulge my wanderlust, but I'm also creating incredible memories with each grandchild and teaching them about different cultures and ways of life."

Linda's approach demonstrates how personal passions can be adapted to include grandchildren, creating unique bonding experiences and educational opportunities. David, a dedicated volunteer at a local animal shelter, initially worried about maintaining his commitment after becoming a grandfather. He was concerned that the time demands of grandparenting would force him to give up his volunteer work, which was a significant part of his identity and sense of purpose.

David found a solution by occasionally bringing his older grandchildren to the shelter with him. "I was nervous at first about how the kids would react to the shelter environment," David recalls. "But they've embraced it wholeheartedly. We've had amazing conversations about animal welfare, responsibility, and the importance of giving back to the community. It's opened their eyes to issues they might not have considered otherwise, and it's given us a shared passion."

By involving his grandchildren in his volunteer work, David not only maintained his personal commitment but also imparted valuable lessons about community service and animal care.

These examples illustrate that with creativity and planning, it's possible to maintain personal interests while also being an involved grandparent. The key lies in finding ways to integrate these interests into your grandparenting role or carve out dedicated time for personal pursuits.

Integrating Grandchildren into Personal Activities

Including grandchildren in your personal interests can be a wonderful way to bond and share your passions. However, it's important to approach this integration thoughtfully and with consideration for the child's age, interests, and abilities.

Here are some detailed strategies for successfully integrating grandchildren into your personal activities:

Age-Appropriate Involvement: Tailor the level of involvement to the child's age and abilities. For younger children, this might mean simplifying activities or focusing on specific aspects they can manage. For example, if you're a passionate gardener, you might have a toddler grandchild help with watering plants or digging small holes, while an older child might help with planting seeds or learning about different plant species.

Margaret, a grandmother of five ranging from ages 3 to 15, shares her experience: "I love quilting, and I've found ways to involve all my grandkids, regardless of their age. The youngest ones helped me choose colors and patterns, the middle ones learned simple stitching, and my oldest granddaughter is now working on her own quilt project. It's amazing to see how their skills and interests grow over time."

Share Your Enthusiasm: Explain why you love your hobby or interest. Your passion can be contagious and might spark a similar interest in your grandchildren. Don't be afraid to show your excitement and share stories about your experiences.

James, a grandfather with a passion for astronomy, found that sharing his enthusiasm made a big difference in engaging his grandchildren. "When I first tried to get the kids interested in stargazing, they were a bit bored. But then I started telling them about the myths behind the constellations and showing them pictures of nebulae and galaxies. Suddenly, they were fascinated. Now, our stargazing nights are a regular event they look forward to."

Be Patient: Remember that children may not immediately share your enthusiasm. Allow them to explore and engage at their own pace. It's important not to force your interests on them but to create opportunities for them to discover these interests naturally.

Lisa, an avid bird watcher, learned this lesson when introducing her hobby to her grandchildren. "At first, the kids found it boring to sit quietly and watch for birds. So, instead of insisting they join me, I started by just pointing out interesting birds when we were out walking or playing. Gradually, they became more curious and started asking questions. Now, two of my grandkids have their own bird guides and binoculars."

Make it Fun: Find ways to make your interests engaging for children. This might involve turning activities into games, incorporating technology, or finding aspects of your hobby that naturally appeal to children.

Michael, a history buff, found creative ways to engage his grandchildren in his passion. "I started by creating scavenger hunts at local historical sites. The kids loved running around looking for specific artifacts or architectural features. From there, we moved on to historical reenactments and even started a family history project together. By making it interactive and fun, they've developed their own love for history."

Balance Shared and Separate Time: While it's great to involve grandchildren in your interests, also maintain some time to pursue these activities on your own or with peers. This balance is important for your own enjoyment and personal growth.

Carol, a grandmother who loves painting, explains how she maintains this balance: "I have a weekly painting class that's just for me. It's my time to focus on my own projects and socialize with other adults who share my interests. But I also have a monthly 'art day' with my grandkids, where we experiment with different techniques and materials.

Having both these outlets keeps my passion fresh and allows me to share it in a meaningful way with the kids."

By thoughtfully integrating your grandchildren into your personal activities, you create opportunities for deeper bonding, skill-sharing, and mutual learning. However, it's equally important to maintain some separate time for your interests. This balance allows you to continue growing personally while also fostering meaningful connections with your grandchildren.

As Keyton (2019) advises, "Finding balance and building boundaries is key to modern grandparenting. It's about creating a harmony between your personal pursuits and your role as a grandparent" (Keyton, 2019). This balance not only enriches your own life but also provides a powerful example to your grandchildren about the importance of maintaining personal interests throughout life.

Remember, the goal is not to force your interests onto your grandchildren but to create opportunities for shared experiences and potential new passions. By maintaining your own hobbies and interests, you continue to grow as an individual, which in turn enhances your ability to be a positive influence in your grandchildren's lives.

Setting Boundaries

Setting healthy boundaries is a crucial aspect of maintaining a balanced life and avoiding burnout as a grandparent. It's important to remember that setting boundaries is not about limiting love or care but about ensuring that you can sustainably provide the best care and support for your grandchildren and their parents. Boundaries help define what you're comfortable with in terms of time, energy, and resources devoted to grandparenting. They also help establish clear expectations for all family members, reducing the likelihood of misunderstandings or resentments.

The Importance of Boundaries

As Morethangrand (2023a) points out, "Grandparents caring for their grandchildren can experience burnout if they don't set clear boundaries and take time for self-care" (morethangrand, 2023a). This observation underscores the critical nature of establishing and maintaining healthy boundaries from the outset of your grandparenting journey.

Boundaries serve multiple purposes in the grandparent-family dynamic:

- **Preventing Burnout:** Without clear boundaries, grandparents may find themselves overextended, leading to physical and emotional exhaustion. This can ultimately diminish the quality of care and interaction they can provide to their grandchildren.

- **Maintaining Personal Identity:** Boundaries help grandparents maintain their sense of self outside of their grandparenting role. This is crucial for personal fulfillment and mental health.

- **Fostering Respect:** Clear boundaries demonstrate self-respect and teach children and adult children to respect others' limits and needs.

- **Reducing Conflict:** When expectations are clearly communicated through boundaries, it reduces the likelihood of misunderstandings and conflicts within the family.

- **Modeling Healthy Relationships:** By setting and maintaining boundaries, grandparents model healthy relationship skills for both their adult children and grandchildren.

Strategies for Communicating Boundaries

Communicating boundaries effectively requires clarity, respect, and, sometimes, diplomacy. Here are some detailed strategies for setting and communicating boundaries with your family:

- **Be Clear and Specific:** Instead of making vague statements, be specific about your boundaries. For example, rather than saying, "I need more time for myself," you might say, "I'm available to babysit on Tuesdays and Thursdays, but I need the other weekdays for my personal activities." This clarity leaves no room for misinterpretation and helps your family understand exactly what you're comfortable with.

- **Use "I" Statements:** Frame your boundaries in terms of your needs rather than as criticisms. For instance, "I feel overwhelmed when I'm asked to babysit at the last minute. I'd appreciate at least a day's notice when possible." This approach focuses on your feelings and needs rather than placing blame, which can help prevent defensive reactions.

- **Be Consistent:** Once you've set a boundary, it's crucial to stick to it. Inconsistency can lead to confusion and may encourage others to push against your boundaries. If you make exceptions, be clear about why and that it doesn't change the overall boundary.

- **Listen and Compromise:** While it's important to maintain your boundaries, also be open to hearing your family's needs and finding compromises where possible. This shows that you're willing to be flexible within reason and can help maintain positive relationships.

- **Review and Adjust:** As circumstances change, be willing to review and adjust your boundaries as needed. What works when grandchildren are toddlers may need to be adjusted as they enter school or become teenagers.

Examples of Healthy Boundary-Setting in Different Family Dynamics

Every family is unique, and boundary-setting may look different depending on your specific situation. Let's explore some detailed examples of healthy boundary-setting in various family dynamics:

The Local Grandparents: Emily and Mike live in the same city as their daughter and her family. They love being involved in their grandchildren's lives but find themselves feeling overwhelmed by frequent last-minute requests for childcare. They set a boundary of needing at least 24 hours' notice for babysitting requests, except in emergencies.

Emily shares, "At first, we were saying yes to every request because we wanted to be helpful. But we found ourselves canceling our own plans and feeling resentful. Now, with the 24-hour notice rule, we can plan our week better and still be there for our family. It's made a huge difference in our stress levels."

This boundary allowed Emily and Mike to maintain their own schedules while still being available to help. It also encouraged their daughter and son-in-law to plan ahead and be more mindful of the grandparents' time.

The Long-Distance Grandparents: Susan and Tom live several states away from their grandchildren. They set a boundary by scheduling regular video calls twice a week rather than being expected to be available for calls at any time.

"We were finding that impromptu calls were often coming at inconvenient times, and we weren't able to give our full attention," Tom explains. "By scheduling regular calls, we ensure that we're fully present and engaged when we talk to our grandkids. It's actually improved the quality of our interactions."

This boundary helped them maintain a connection while also respecting everyone's schedules. It also created a routine that the grandchildren could look forward to.

The Retired Grandparents: Janet and Bob, both retired, were happy to help with childcare but found that it was taking over their lives. They set a boundary of being available for childcare three days a week, leaving the other days for their own activities and interests.

Janet reflects, "We love our grandkids, but we realized we were putting our own lives on hold. By setting specific days for childcare, we've been able to pursue our own interests and maintain our social connections. We find that we're more energetic and engaged with the grandkids on our caregiving days as a result."

This boundary allowed Janet and Bob to enjoy their retirement while still playing a significant role in their grandchildren's lives.

The Working Grandparents: Lisa and Mark are still working full-time but want to be involved in their grandchildren's lives. They set a boundary by being available for weekend activities and occasional evening babysitting but not for regular weekday childcare.

Mark shares, "We had to be upfront about our limitations due to work. We make sure to be fully present during our weekend time with the grandkids, and we're always there for special events or emergencies. Our kids understand that we can't do regular weekday care, and they've made other arrangements for that."

This boundary allowed Lisa and Mark to balance their work commitments with their desire to be involved as grandparents.

The Grandparents with Multiple Grandchildren: Maria and John have five grandchildren from their three adult children. They set a boundary of rotating their time and attention among the families to ensure fairness and manage their energy levels.

Maria explains, "With five grandkids, we were feeling pulled in all directions. We created a rotation system where we focus on one family each week for special activities or babysitting. Of course, we're flexible for birthdays or special events, but this system has helped us give quality time to each grandchild without burning out."

This boundary helped Maria and John manage their energy and ensure that each grandchild received focused attention.

In each of these cases, setting clear boundaries allowed the grandparents to be involved and supportive while also maintaining their own well-being and personal lives. It's important to note that setting boundaries is an ongoing process that may require adjustment over time as circumstances change.

As Compass (2024) advises, "Setting boundaries with adult children and grandchildren is about creating a healthy family dynamic where everyone's needs are respected. It's not about creating distance, but about fostering respectful, loving relationships" (Compass, 2024).

Remember, effective boundary-setting is a skill that can be developed over time. It may feel uncomfortable at first, especially if you're not used to asserting your own needs. However, with practice and clear communication, boundaries can significantly improve your relationships and overall well-being as a grandparent.

Chapter 6:
Supporting New Parents

Becoming a grandparent is an exciting and joyous experience, but it also comes with the responsibility of supporting your adult children as they navigate the challenges of new parenthood. This chapter will provide grandparents with helpful strategies to assist new parents while respecting their boundaries, ensuring a harmonious family dynamic.

Offering Practical Support

One of the most valuable ways grandparents can help new parents is by offering practical support. This can take many forms, from cooking meals to babysitting. However, it's essential to balance being helpful and overbearing.

Cooking meals is indeed one of the most appreciated forms of support. New parents often struggle to find time to prepare nutritious meals while caring for a newborn. By providing home-cooked meals, grandparents can ensure the new parents are well-nourished during this demanding time. Sarah, a grandmother of two, shares her experience: "When my daughter had her first baby, I was so excited to help. I started by cooking meals and bringing them over. I remember the relief on my daughter's face when she realized she didn't have to worry about dinner for the first week. It was a small gesture, but it made a big difference."

This simple act of cooking can have a profound impact on new parents' well-being. It not only provides them with necessary nutrition but also gives them one less thing to worry about during an overwhelming time. Consider preparing meals that are easy to reheat or can be frozen for later use. This approach ensures that the parents can access nutritious food even when they're not there.

Babysitting is another crucial form of support. As Seyedi (2022) advises, "Offer to watch the baby for a few hours so the new parents can catch up on sleep, run errands, or simply have some time to themselves" (Seyedi, 2022). This respite can be invaluable for new parents who are often sleep-deprived and overwhelmed.

John, a grandfather of three, recalls: "I remember offering to watch my grandson for a few hours so my son and daughter-in-law could go out for dinner. It was their first date night since the baby was born, and they came back looking refreshed and happy. It made me realize how important it is for new parents to have some time to reconnect as a couple."

When babysitting, it's important to follow the parents' instructions closely. This includes adhering to feeding schedules, sleep routines, and any specific care instructions they've provided. By doing so, you're not only helping the parents but also maintaining consistency for the baby, which is crucial for their development and well-being.

Being Present Without Dominating

While being present and available is crucial, it's equally important not to dominate or take over. New parents need space to learn and grow into their new roles. As AMALAH (2010) suggests, "Be helpful, but don't hover. New parents need to figure things out for themselves, too" (AMALAH, 2010).

This balance can be challenging to achieve, especially when you see your adult children struggling with the challenges of new parenthood. It's natural to want to step in and take over, drawing from your own experiences as a parent. However, it's crucial to remember that parenting practices and recommendations have likely changed since you raised your children.

Linda, a grandmother of four, shares her approach: "I learned to ask, 'How can I help?' instead of assuming I knew what was needed. Sometimes, my daughter just wanted me to sit with her while she nursed the baby. Other times, she needed me to do laundry or tidy up. By asking, I could be truly helpful without overstepping." This approach of asking rather than assuming is key to providing support without dominating. It allows the new parents to maintain their autonomy and decision-making role while still benefiting from your help. It also shows respect for their parenting choices and methods, which may differ from your own.

Small Gestures That Make a Big Difference

Often, it's the small gestures that can make the biggest impact. These can include running errands, doing household chores, or providing emotional support. These seemingly minor acts of kindness can significantly alleviate the stress and overwhelm that new parents often experience.

Running errands, such as picking up groceries, diapers, or other necessities, can be a huge help. New parents, especially in the early weeks, may find it challenging to leave the house with a newborn. By offering to pick up essentials, you're saving them time, energy, and stress. Doing household chores is another way to provide valuable support. Taking care of laundry, dishes, or light cleaning can alleviate stress for new parents who are likely struggling to keep up with household tasks while caring for a newborn. Tom, a new grandfather, shares: "I noticed my son's house was getting a bit messy when I visited. Without saying anything, I started doing small chores each time I came, overloading the dishwasher, folding laundry, or tidying up the living room. My son later told me how much he appreciated it, as it was one less thing for them to worry about."

Emotional support is perhaps one of the most crucial forms of help you can offer. Sometimes, just being there to listen and offer encouragement can be incredibly valuable. New parents often grapple with feelings of inadequacy, exhaustion, and overwhelming responsibility. Your presence and reassurance can make a world of difference.

Maria, a new grandmother, shares: "I remember my daughter breaking down in tears one day, feeling overwhelmed. I just held her and listened. Later, she told me that moment of support meant more to her than any practical help I could have offered."

This emotional support can take many forms. It might be listening without judgment when they express frustrations or doubts. It could be sharing your own experiences of early parenthood, not as a way to give unsolicited advice but to reassure them that what they're feeling is normal and that it does get easier. It might also involve being a cheerleader, celebrating their small victories, and reassuring them that they're doing a great job.

Creating a Supportive Environment

Beyond these specific forms of support, grandparents can play a crucial role in creating a supportive environment for new parents. This involves being a positive presence in their lives and fostering a sense of confidence in their parenting abilities.

One way to do this is by offering genuine praise and encouragement. Notice and comment on the things they're doing well as parents. This positive reinforcement can boost their confidence and help them feel more capable in their new roles.

Kate, a grandmother of two, shares her approach: "I make a point of telling my daughter how well she's doing as a mom. I point out specific things I notice - how patient she is during feeding times, how she soothes the baby so well, and how organized she is with the baby's schedule. I can see how these words of affirmation boost her confidence."

Another aspect of creating a supportive environment is respecting the new family unit. This means recognizing that your adult child and their partner are now the primary decision-makers when it comes to their child. It involves respecting their parenting choices, even if they differ from what you would do.

James, a new grandfather, reflects: "When my son and daughter-in-law decided to use cloth diapers, I was skeptical. But instead of voicing my doubts, I asked them to explain their decision and show me how it worked. By showing interest and respect for their choice, I felt like I was supporting them in their parenting journey, even if it was different from how we did things."

Adapting to Modern Parenting Practices

One challenge many grandparents face is adapting to modern parenting practices that may differ significantly from what was common when they were raising children. It's important to stay open-minded and willing to learn about current recommendations and trends in childcare.

This might involve educating yourself about current safety guidelines, feeding practices, or sleep recommendations. The NCT (National Childbirth Trust) (2023) advises, "Try to keep an open mind about different approaches to parenting. Things may have changed since you were a new parent" (NCT, 2023).

By staying informed and adaptable, you can provide support that aligns with the parents' chosen methods and current best practices. This not only ensures the baby's safety and well-being but also shows respect for the parents' choices and helps maintain a harmonious relationship.

Remember, your role as a grandparent is to support and complement the parents' efforts, not to replace or undermine them. By offering practical help, providing emotional support, and creating a supportive environment while respecting boundaries, you can play a vital role in supporting new parents through the challenges and joys of early parenthood.

Honoring Parental Decisions

Respecting Parenting Choices

One of the most critical aspects of supporting new parents is honoring their choices and approaches to parenting. This can be challenging, especially when their methods differ from how you raised your children. As grandparents, it's natural to draw from our own experiences and want to share our knowledge. However, it's crucial to remember that parenting practices evolve over time, and what worked for us may not be the best approach today.

As Janet Lansbury (2011) points out, "It's important to remember that parenting styles evolve, and what worked for us may not be the best approach today" (Lansbury, 2011). This perspective is crucial in maintaining a supportive relationship with your adult children. It requires a willingness to set aside our preconceptions and be open to new ideas and methods.

Tom, a grandfather of two, shares his experience: "When my son decided to use cloth diapers, I was skeptical. It seemed like so much extra work. But I bit my tongue and decided to learn about it instead of criticizing. Now, I'm amazed at how far cloth diapering has come, and I'm proud of my son for making an environmentally conscious choice."

Tom's experience illustrates the importance of keeping an open mind and being willing to learn about new parenting practices. By choosing to educate himself rather than criticize, he not only supported his son's decision but also strengthened their relationship and gained new knowledge himself.

Respecting parenting choices goes beyond just accepting them; it involves actively supporting and reinforcing these choices when you're caring for your grandchildren. This might mean following specific feeding schedules, adhering to sleep routines, or using particular disciplinary approaches that the parents have chosen.

Maria, a grandmother of three, shares her approach: "My daughter practices gentle parenting, which is very different from how I raised her. At first, I found it challenging not to intervene in ways I was used to. But I've learned to follow her lead, using the phrases and techniques she uses with the children. It's been a learning experience for me, and I can see how it positively affects the children." This kind of active support not only helps maintain consistency for the grandchildren but also demonstrates respect for the parents' choices and authority.

It shows that you value their decisions and are willing to adapt your behavior to support their parenting style.

Dealing with Divergent Parenting Ideologies

When faced with parenting approaches that differ from your own, it's essential to stay open-minded, educate yourself, and offer support rather than criticism. This can be particularly challenging when you have strong opinions or concerns about certain practices.

Staying open-minded involves trying to understand the reasoning behind their choices. Often, new parenting practices are based on recent research or an evolving understanding of child development. By approaching these differences with curiosity rather than judgment, you can learn about the benefits of these new approaches.

Karen, a grandmother of three, recalls: "When my daughter decided to practice baby-led weaning, I was terrified. I was sure the baby would choke. But instead of voicing my fears, I asked her to explain the method to me and show me how to do it safely. Now, I'm amazed at how well it works, and I feel more connected to my daughter because I took the time to understand her choice."

Karen's experience highlights the importance of education in dealing with divergent parenting ideologies. By taking the time to learn about baby-led weaning, she was able to overcome her initial fears and support her daughter's choice. This approach not only helped her understand and accept the new method but also strengthened her relationship with her daughter. Educating yourself about modern parenting practices and the research behind them is crucial. This might involve reading books or articles on current parenting trends, attending parenting classes with your adult children, or even consulting with pediatricians or child development experts. By staying informed, you can engage in more meaningful conversations about parenting choices and offer more relevant support. John, a grandfather of two, shares his experience: "When my daughter told me she was planning a home birth, I was initially very concerned. But instead of immediately expressing my worries, I decided to research it. I read studies about home birth safety, talked to midwives, and even watched documentaries about it. By the time my granddaughter was born, I felt much more comfortable with the idea and was able to be a supportive presence during the birth."

Offering support, not criticism, is perhaps the most crucial aspect of dealing with divergent parenting ideologies. Even if you disagree with certain choices, focusing on supporting your adult children's decisions can help maintain a positive relationship and ensure you remain a trusted part of your grandchildren's lives.

This doesn't mean you can never express concerns, but how and when you do so is important. If you have serious worries about a parenting choice, it's best to have a private, calm conversation with the parents, expressing your concerns in a non-judgmental way and being open to hearing their perspectives.

Examples of Considerate and Encouraging Grandparents

Considerate grandparents find ways to support new parents' decisions while offering gentle guidance when asked. This might involve respecting sleep training methods, supporting feeding choices, or adhering to screen time rules. For instance, if parents are using a specific sleep training method, grandparents should follow it consistently when babysitting. This consistency is crucial for the child's routine and shows respect for the parents' choices. Emily, a grandmother of four, shares: "My daughter uses the 'cry it out' method for sleep training, which was hard for me at first. I wanted to rush in and comfort the baby. But I understood how important consistency was, so I followed her instructions exactly. It was challenging, but I knew I was supporting her parenting choice by doing so."

Supporting feeding choices is another area where grandparents can show consideration. Whether parents choose breastfeeding, formula feeding, or a combination, grandparents should offer encouragement and practical support.

Robert, a grandfather of two, recalls: "When my daughter-in-law struggled with breastfeeding, I could see how stressed she was. Instead of suggesting she switch to formula, which is what I wanted to do, I supported her decision by helping in other ways. I'd bring her water and snacks while she was feeding or take the baby for burping afterward. I could see how much she appreciated the support."

Adhering to screen time rules is increasingly important in today's digital age. If parents have strict rules about screen time, grandparents should respect and enforce these rules during visits.

Lisa, a grandmother of two, shares: "My daughter-in-law is very strict about screen time. At first, I thought it was excessive, but I decided to respect her wishes. Instead of turning on the TV when the kids visit, I've rediscovered the joy of board games and outdoor activities. It's actually brought us all closer together."

Lisa's experience shows how respecting parental decisions, even when they differ from our preferences, can lead to positive outcomes. By finding alternative activities, she not only honored the parents' wishes but also created meaningful, screen-free interactions with her grandchildren.

Another area where considerate grandparents can make a difference is in respecting dietary choices. Many parents today have specific dietary preferences for their children, whether for health, ethical, or environmental reasons.

Sarah, a grandmother of three, shares her experience: "My son and daughter-in-law are raising their children vegan. At first, I found it challenging to cook for them or buy appropriate snacks. But I decided to embrace it as a learning opportunity. I've learned so many new recipes and found that I enjoy vegan cooking. It's become a new shared interest between me and my daughter-in-law."

By adapting to the family's dietary choices, Sarah not only showed respect for their decisions but also found a new way to connect with her family.

Encouraging grandparents also find ways to support parents' choices without overstepping boundaries. This might involve offering praise for their parenting approaches, showing interest in their methods, or simply being a non-judgmental listener when they want to discuss their parenting journey.

James, a grandfather of one, shares: "I make a point of telling my son how impressed I am with his parenting. I notice things like how patient he is during tantrums or how he always gets down to the child's level when talking. Even if it's different from how I parented, I can see it's effective, and I make sure to say so."

This kind of positive reinforcement can be incredibly valuable for new parents who may be feeling unsure or overwhelmed. By focusing on the positives and offering encouragement, grandparents can boost parents' confidence and strengthen family relationships.

Improving Communication

The Importance of Open and Honest Communication

Open and honest communication forms the bedrock of a strong relationship between grandparents and new parents. It serves multiple crucial functions: preventing misunderstandings, resolving conflicts, and ensuring that everyone's needs are met. In the context of grandparenting, this kind of communication becomes even more vital as families navigate the complex dynamics of multigenerational relationships.

As Debbie Pincus (2024) astutely observes, "Good communication involves both speaking up about your own needs and listening to understand the other person's perspective" (Pincus, 2024). This insight highlights the two-way nature of effective communication. It's not just about expressing your thoughts and feelings but also actively listening and seeking to understand the viewpoint of others.

For grandparents, this might mean clearly expressing your desire to be involved in your grandchild's life while also listening to and respecting the boundaries that new parents may set. For new parents, it could involve sharing their parenting philosophies and expectations while also being open to the wisdom and experience that grandparents can offer.

Sarah, a grandmother of three, shares her experience: "When my first grandchild was born, I was so excited that I wanted to be there all the time. But I quickly realized that my daughter and son-in-law needed space to figure things out on their own.

We had an open conversation where I expressed my enthusiasm, and they shared their need for some independence. By talking it through, we found a balance that worked for everyone."

This example illustrates how open communication can lead to mutually satisfactory solutions, even when initial desires or expectations may differ.

Techniques for Having Difficult Conversations

Despite the best intentions, sometimes difficult conversations are necessary. These might arise from differences in parenting philosophies, perceived overstepping of boundaries, or misunderstandings about roles and expectations. While these conversations can be challenging, they are often crucial for maintaining healthy family relationships.

When approaching these discussions, it's important to choose the right time and place. Ensure you have privacy and enough time to discuss the issue thoroughly without interruptions. This might mean scheduling a specific time to talk when children are not present, allowing for a focused and unrushed conversation.

Using "I" statements is another valuable technique. Instead of saying, "You always interfere with my parenting," try, "I feel frustrated when my parenting decisions are questioned." This approach expresses your feelings without blaming or accusing, which can help prevent the other person from becoming defensive.

Active listening is a crucial skill in these conversations. Pay attention to what the other person is saying without interrupting or planning your response. This shows respect and a genuine desire to understand their perspective.

Mark, a grandfather of four, shares his experience with a difficult conversation: "When I disagreed with how my son was disciplining his children, I knew I had to address it. I waited until we were alone and calmly expressed my concerns. I made sure to listen to his reasoning, and we had a productive discussion. We didn't agree on everything, but we understood each other better afterward."

Mark's approach demonstrates several key techniques: choosing the right time, expressing concerns calmly, and listening to understand. Even though the complete agreement wasn't reached, the conversation improved mutual understanding, which is often the most realistic and beneficial outcome of such discussions.

Seeking to understand is another crucial aspect of these conversations. Ask questions to clarify the other person's perspective. This not only helps you gain a better understanding but also shows that you value their viewpoint.

Finally, focus on solutions rather than dwelling on problems. Work together to find a resolution that addresses everyone's concerns. This collaborative approach can strengthen relationships even as you work through difficulties.

Soriah Mitchell (2019) offers valuable advice, suggesting that we "Approach difficult conversations with a mindset of curiosity and collaboration, rather than confrontation" (Mitchell, 2019). This mindset shift can dramatically change the tone and outcome of challenging discussions.

Effective Communication Strategies

Beyond techniques for difficult conversations, several strategies can enhance day-to-day communication between grandparents and new parents.

Regular check-ins can be incredibly valuable. Establish a routine of checking in with new parents to see how they're doing and what they need. This could be a weekly phone call or a regular coffee date. These check-ins provide an opportunity for ongoing, open communication and allow you to stay connected with the family's evolving needs.

Linda, a grandmother of two, shares: "Every Sunday evening, I have a quick call with my daughter. Sometimes, it's just to say hello; other times, we discuss upcoming plans or any concerns. This regular contact helps us stay connected and address any issues before they become big problems."

Being specific in your offers of help is another effective strategy. Instead of saying "Let me know if you need anything," which puts the onus on the new parents to ask for help, offer specific forms of assistance. For example, you might say, "I'd like to bring over a home-cooked meal this week. Would Tuesday or Thursday be better for you?"

Respecting boundaries is crucial for maintaining good communication. If parents set certain rules or boundaries, acknowledge and respect them. This shows that you value their parenting decisions and helps build trust.

Expressing appreciation is a simple yet powerful communication strategy. Recognize and appreciate the efforts of new parents. This could be as simple as saying, "I've noticed how patient you are with the baby. You're doing a great job."

Emily, a new mother, shares how her parents' communication style has been helpful: "My parents always ask before they come over, and they're great at reading the room. If I seem stressed, they offer to take the baby for a walk. If I'm lonely, they sit and chat with me. Their ability to tune into what I need without me having to spell it out has been incredible."

This example highlights the importance of emotional intelligence in communication. By being attuned to Emily's needs and moods, her parents can offer appropriate support without her having to explicitly ask for it.

Special Circumstances: Supporting Parents of NICU Babies

When a grandchild is in the Neonatal Intensive Care Unit (NICU), grandparents face unique challenges in providing support. The NICU experience can be overwhelming, frightening, and emotionally draining for new parents. In these circumstances, effective communication becomes even more crucial.

As Smith (2013) points out, "The NICU experience can be overwhelming for new parents, and grandparents play a crucial role in providing emotional and practical support during this difficult time" (Smith, 2013). This support, however, must be carefully calibrated to the needs and wishes of the parents.

Offering emotional support is perhaps the most important role grandparents can play in this situation. Be a listening ear and a shoulder to cry on. Allow the parents to express their fears, frustrations, and hopes without judgment. Sometimes, a silent presence is the most powerful form of support.

Helping with practical tasks can also be invaluable. Offer to do laundry, prepare meals, or take care of pets. These tasks, which can seem overwhelming to parents focused on their NICU baby, can provide significant relief.

If there are other children in the family, offering to care for them can allow parents to focus on the NICU baby. This support can help maintain some normalcy for siblings and reduce stress for the parents.

Educating yourself about the baby's condition and the NICU environment is another way to provide support. This knowledge can help you understand what the family is going through and may allow you to ask informed questions or provide more targeted support.

Respecting visiting rules is crucial in the NICU setting. Follow the NICU's guidelines for visitors and respect the parent's wishes regarding visits. Some parents may want the support of having grandparents present, while others may need space to bond with their baby.

Linda, a grandmother whose grandson was in the NICU for six weeks, shares: "It was a scary time for all of us. I found that the best thing I could do was to be there for my daughter and son-in-law. I'd bring them home-cooked meals at the hospital, sit with them during long waits, and take care of things at home so they could focus on their baby. It was hard seeing them go through this, but being able to support them made me feel useful during a time when we all felt so helpless."

Linda's experience illustrates how practical support, emotional presence, and respect for the parents' needs can make a significant difference during the challenging NICU experience.

In all these communication strategies, the key is to remain flexible, empathetic, and respectful. Every family's needs and dynamics are different, and what works in one situation may not work in another. By maintaining open lines of communication, grandparents can provide valuable support to new parents while nurturing strong, positive relationships with both their adult children and their grandchildren.

Chapter 7:
Establishing a Network of Grandparents

Becoming a grandparent is a transformative experience that brings joy, challenges, and a new perspective on life. While the focus is often on the relationship between grandparents and their grandchildren, the importance of connecting with other grandparents cannot be overstated. This chapter will guide you on how to find other grandparents to lean on for advice, cheer you on, and share life stories with, creating a supportive network that enhances your grandparenting journey.

The Benefits of Connecting with Other Grandparents

Shared Experiences and Emotional Support

One of the primary benefits of connecting with other grandparents is the opportunity to share experiences and receive emotional support. As GrandkidsMatter (2020) points out, "Grandparenting creates magical connections and very real benefits, not just for grandchildren but for grandparents as well" (GrandkidsMatter, 2020). These connections extend beyond the family unit to include relationships with other grandparents who understand the unique joys and challenges of this role.

The emotional support gained from these connections can be invaluable. Grandparents often face a range of emotions, from overwhelming joy to uncertainty about their new role. Having a network of peers who are going through similar experiences provides a safe space to express these feelings and gain reassurance.

Martha, a grandmother of three, shares her experience: "When I first became a grandmother, I felt overwhelmed with emotions – excitement, love, but also uncertainty about my new role. Joining a local grandparent group was a game-changer. Suddenly, I had a whole network of people who understood exactly what I was going through. We laugh together, support each other through challenges, and celebrate our grandchildren's milestones. It's like having an extended family."

Martha's experience highlights how connecting with other grandparents can provide a sense of community and belonging. This network becomes a source of shared joy during happy moments and a support system during challenging times. Whether it's celebrating a grandchild's first steps or navigating the complexities of long-distance grandparenting, having peers who understand these experiences can be immensely comforting.

Learning and Growth Opportunities

Connecting with other grandparents also provides valuable learning and growth opportunities. Each grandparent brings their own experiences, knowledge, and perspectives to the table, creating a rich environment for sharing wisdom and learning new approaches to grandparenting.

As Elliot Marcille (2017) notes, "The benefit of collective wisdom cannot be overstated. When we come together and share our experiences, we create a knowledge base far greater than any individual could possess" (Marcille, 2017). This collective wisdom can be particularly valuable for grandparents navigating the ever-changing landscape of modern parenting and family dynamics.

These learning opportunities can cover a wide range of topics. Grandparents might share tips on bonding with grandchildren of different ages, navigating relationships with adult children, or staying connected in the digital age. They might exchange ideas for activities, discuss current parenting trends, or share resources they've found helpful.

John, a grandfather of two, recalls: "I was struggling with how to connect with my tech-savvy teenage grandson. At a grandparent meetup, another grandfather shared how he learned to play online games with his grandkids. It opened up a whole new way for me to bond with my grandson. I never would have thought of it on my own, but now we have weekly gaming sessions that we both look forward to."

John's experience illustrates how the collective wisdom of a grandparent network can lead to innovative solutions to common challenges. By sharing their experiences, grandparents can help each other adapt to the changing needs of their grandchildren and stay relevant in their lives.

Combating Isolation and Promoting Well-being

For many, grandparenthood can sometimes feel isolating, especially if friends and peers aren't at the same life stage. Building a network of grandparents can combat this isolation and promote overall well-being. The transition to grandparenthood often coincides with other life changes, such as retirement or reduced work hours. While these changes can provide more time for family, they can also lead to a sense of loss of purpose or social connection. Connecting with other grandparents can provide a new social outlet and a sense of purpose beyond family roles.

The Russley Village (2020) emphasizes that "the grandparent's role in society is highly valued, contributing to both family dynamics and personal fulfillment" (The Russley Village, 2020). By connecting with other grandparents, individuals can reinforce this sense of value and purpose while also maintaining active social lives.

Linda, a grandmother of one, shares: "After retiring, I found myself with a lot of free time. Becoming a grandmother was wonderful, but I still felt like something was missing. Joining a grandparent group filled that gap. Now, I have regular social outings, volunteer opportunities, and a sense of community that goes beyond my role as a grandmother. It's enriched my life in ways I never expected."

Linda's story demonstrates how connecting with other grandparents can provide a sense of community and purpose that extends beyond family roles. These connections can lead to new friendships, shared interests, and opportunities for personal growth and contribution to the community.

Finding and Joining Grandparent Groups

Local Community Groups

Many communities have local grandparent groups that meet regularly. These can be found in community centers, libraries, or religious organizations. Local groups offer the advantage of face-to-face interactions and the potential for developing close, in-person friendships.

To find these groups, start by checking local community bulletin boards or newspapers for announcements. Many libraries and community centers have dedicated spaces for posting information about local groups and events. Don't hesitate to inquire at your local senior center or YMCA about grandparent programs. These organizations often host or have information about various community groups, including those for grandparents.

If you're part of a religious community, ask at your place of worship if they have any grandparent ministries or groups. Many religious organizations recognize the unique role of grandparents and offer support groups or social gatherings specifically for them.

Sarah, a grandmother of four, found her group through an unexpected source: "I was at the library with my youngest grandchild for storytime, and I noticed a flyer for a grandparent coffee morning. I decided to give it a try, and it's become a highlight of my week. We meet every Tuesday, share stories, and often have speakers on topics relevant to grandparenting."

Sarah's experience shows how local groups can become a regular and enriching part of a grandparent's life. These groups often evolve to meet the needs of their members, offering a mix of social interaction, support, and educational opportunities.

Online Communities

In today's digital age, online communities provide a convenient way to connect with other grandparents, regardless of geographical location. These communities can be especially valuable for grandparents who live in rural areas, have mobility issues, or simply prefer the flexibility of online interaction.

Paulina Colwell (2017) provides an extensive list of grandparent blogs and websites that can serve as starting points for finding online communities (Colwell, 2017). These online resources often have associated forums or social media groups where grandparents can connect and interact.

Facebook Groups are a popular platform for grandparent networking. There are numerous groups dedicated to grandparenting, ranging from general discussion groups to those focused on specific aspects of grandparenting, such as long-distance relationships or grandparenting children with special needs. To find these groups, try searching for terms like "Grandparents Group" or "Grandparent Support" in the Facebook search bar.

Forums on websites like GransNet or AARP's Grandparenting Forum offer spaces for grandparents to connect, ask questions, and share experiences. These forums often have different sections for various topics, allowing grandparents to find discussions relevant to their specific situation or interests.

Following and engaging with grandparenting blogs can provide both information and community. Many bloggers foster a sense of community among their readers through comment sections or associated social media groups.

Tom, a tech-savvy grandfather of three, shares his online experience: "I joined a Facebook group for grandparents, and it's been incredible. We share photos, ask for advice, and even organize virtual meetups. It's especially great for connecting with grandparents who have grandkids the same age as mine. We exchange tips on age-appropriate activities and gifts."

Tom's experience highlights how online communities can provide both practical support and social connection. These groups allow grandparents to tap into a wide range of experiences and perspectives, often in real-time.

Grandparent Classes and Workshops

Many hospitals, community colleges, and family support organizations offer classes or workshops for grandparents. These can be excellent opportunities to learn and connect with others who are at a similar stage in their grandparenting journey. These classes often cover a range of topics relevant to modern grandparenting, such as current childcare practices, safety guidelines, and navigating family dynamics. They provide not only valuable information but also a structured environment for meeting other grandparents.

Mary, a first-time grandmother, recalls: "I attended a 'New Grandparent Boot Camp' at our local hospital. Not only did I learn a lot about current childcare practices, but I also met a group of grandparents-to-be who were just as excited and nervous as I was. We've kept in touch and now have regular playdates with our grandkids."

Mary's experience shows how these classes can be the starting point for lasting connections. The shared experience of learning together often creates a bond that extends beyond the classroom, leading to ongoing friendships and support networks.

Sharing Resources and Collective Wisdom

Once you've established connections with other grandparents, the sharing of resources and collective wisdom becomes an invaluable aspect of these relationships. This exchange of knowledge, experiences, and practical tips can significantly enhance your grandparenting journey, providing fresh perspectives and solutions to common challenges.

Exchanging Tips and Activities

Grandparents often possess a wealth of knowledge when it comes to activities and games that children enjoy. Sharing these ideas within your grandparent network can provide everyone with fresh, engaging ways to connect with their grandchildren. This exchange is particularly valuable as it allows grandparents to stay current with the interests of younger generations while also passing on timeless activities that have brought joy across generations.

Pat Rumbaugh (2018) suggests several activities for grandparents and grandchildren to enjoy together, such as nature walks, cooking, or creating family history projects (Rumbaugh, 2018). These ideas can serve as starting points for discussions and exchanges within your grandparent network.

Nature walks, for instance, can be adapted to suit various ages and locations. Younger children might enjoy a simple scavenger hunt in a local park, while older grandchildren might be interested in bird watching or learning about local flora. Cooking together not only creates delicious treats but also provides opportunities to pass down family recipes and teach valuable life skills. Family history projects can range from creating simple family trees with younger grandchildren to in-depth genealogy research with older ones.

Barbara, a grandmother of five, shares: "In our grandparent group, we have a monthly 'idea exchange' where everyone brings an activity they've enjoyed with their grandkids. I learned how to make slime, which my grandkids love, and I shared my secret for the perfect blanket fort. It's wonderful to have this constant source of new ideas."

Barbara's experience highlights the dynamic nature of these exchanges. While traditional activities like building blanket forts remain popular, grandparents also need to keep up with modern trends like slime-making. This blend of old and new activities ensures that grandparents can engage with their grandchildren on multiple levels. These exchanges can cover a wide range of topics beyond just activities. Grandparents might share tips on handling behavioral issues, navigating technology with grandchildren, or finding age-appropriate books and educational resources. They might discuss strategies for maintaining connections with long-distance grandchildren or ways to support grandchildren with special needs.

For example, Tom, a grandfather of three, shares his tech tip: "I was struggling to keep up with my grandkids' video game talk. Another grandparent in our group suggested I watch gaming YouTube channels to learn the basics. Now, I can have real conversations with my grandsons about their favorite games, even if I don't play them myself."

The Value of Shared Experiences

Darian Krey (2020) emphasizes "the value of shared experience" in building connections and understanding (Krey, 2020). Within a grandparent network, these shared experiences can provide comfort, validation, and new perspectives. This sharing of experiences goes beyond just exchanging practical tips; it creates a supportive environment where grandparents can openly discuss their joys, challenges, and concerns.

Frank, a grandfather of two, recalls: "When my daughter announced she was moving across the country with my grandkids, I was devastated. At our grandparent group meeting, I shared my feelings, and to my surprise, two other members had gone through similar situations. They offered advice on maintaining long-distance relationships with grandkids that I never would have thought of on my own. Their support made a difficult situation much more manageable."

Frank's experience illustrates how shared experiences can provide emotional support and practical solutions. In his case, the shared experience of long-distance grandparenting led to valuable advice on maintaining strong relationships despite physical distance. This might have included tips on using technology for regular video calls, sending care packages, or planning special activities for visits.

These shared experiences can cover a wide range of situations that grandparents might face. For instance, grandparents might discuss how they've navigated disagreements with their adult children over parenting styles, how they've adapted to changing family dynamics after a divorce, or how they've found ways to bond with grandchildren of different ages.

Linda, a grandmother of four, shares: "In our group, we often discuss how to handle situations where our parenting advice isn't welcome. One grandmother shared how she learned to offer support without giving unsolicited advice. Her approach of asking, 'How can I help?' instead of telling her daughter what to do really resonated with me. It's improved my relationship with my own daughter tremendously."

This exchange of experiences not only provides practical strategies but also offers emotional reassurance. Knowing that others have faced similar challenges and found ways to overcome them can be incredibly comforting and empowering for grandparents.

Recommended Resources

Sharing books, articles, and online resources can greatly benefit your grandparent network. These resources can provide expert insights, research-based advice, and a broader perspective on grandparenting in the modern world. Some suggested reads and resources include:

"The Joy of Being a Grandparent" by Susan Adcox: This book offers a comprehensive guide to modern grandparenting, covering topics from bonding with grandchildren to navigating family dynamics. It provides both practical advice and heartwarming stories that many grandparents find relatable and inspiring.

"Good to Be Grand" by Cheryl Harbour: This book offers insights into the changing role of grandparents in today's families. It guides everything from child safety to using technology to connect with grandchildren.

AARP Grandparenting Resources (www.aarp.org/grandparents): This website offers a wealth of articles, videos, and tools for grandparents. Topics range from legal issues affecting grandparents to fun activity ideas for grandchildren of all ages.

Grandparents.com: This website provides articles, advice columns, and forums where grandparents can connect and share experiences. It covers a wide range of topics relevant to modern grandparenting.

In addition to these resources, many grandparents find value in sharing articles from reputable parenting websites, child development resources, or even academic studies related to grandparenting. These can provide evidence-based information to support grandparenting practices.

Sarah, a grandmother of three, shares how resource sharing has benefited her group: "We have a virtual bookshelf where we all add resources we've found helpful. One member shared a fantastic article on helping grandchildren cope with anxiety, which was so relevant given the stresses kids face today. Another shared a podcast series on grandparenting that several of us now listen to regularly. It's like having a curated library of grandparenting wisdom at our fingertips."

Encourage members of your network to share resources they've found helpful, creating a collective library of grandparenting wisdom. This could be as simple as sharing links in a group chat or as organized as creating a shared online document or group Pinterest board with resources.

Remember that while these resources can be incredibly valuable, they should complement, not replace, the personal experiences and wisdom shared within the group. The most powerful learning often comes from combining expert advice with the real-life experiences of fellow grandparents.

John, a grandfather of four, notes: "We often discuss the books or articles we've read in our meetings. It's fascinating to see how different grandparents interpret and apply advice based on their situations. These discussions have helped me realize that there's rarely a one-size-fits-all approach to grandparenting. We need to adapt the advice to our unique family dynamics."

Organizing Gatherings for Grandparents

Organizing regular gatherings can significantly strengthen your grandparent network and provide valuable opportunities for both socializing and support. These gatherings serve as the cornerstone of a thriving grandparent community, offering a space for shared experiences, mutual learning, and the cultivation of meaningful relationships.

Creating a Welcoming Atmosphere

When planning gatherings, it's crucial to create a welcoming and inclusive atmosphere. This involves careful consideration of various factors to ensure that all members feel comfortable, valued, and eager to participate. Choosing accessible locations is a key aspect of creating an inclusive environment. This means selecting venues that are easily reachable by various modes of transportation and are wheelchair accessible if needed. Consider locations with ample parking or proximity to public transportation. Community centers, libraries, or local cafes with private rooms can be excellent choices.

Lisa, who coordinates a local grandparent group, shares her approach: "We make sure everyone feels valued in our group. We rotate meeting locations and times to accommodate different needs. We also have a 'no judgment' rule – everyone's grandparenting journey is unique, and we're here to support, not critique."

Lisa's strategy of rotating meeting locations is particularly effective. It ensures that the burden of travel doesn't always fall on the same members and allows the group to explore different areas of the community. This rotation can also make the gatherings more interesting and varied.

Varying meeting times is another important consideration. Some grandparents might be retired and prefer daytime meetings, while others who are still working might need evening or weekend gatherings. By offering a mix of times, you can ensure that all members have the opportunity to attend regularly.

Tom, a working grandfather, appreciates this flexibility: "Our group alternates between Saturday morning meetings and Wednesday evening gatherings. This means I can always make at least two meetings a month, even with my work schedule. It's made a big difference in helping me feel connected to the group." Encouraging all members to participate and share is vital for creating a sense of belonging within the group. This can be achieved through structured activities that give everyone a chance to speak, such as round-robin sharing sessions or small group discussions.

Sarah, a shy grandmother, found this approach helpful: "At first, I was nervous about speaking up in the large group. However, our coordinator started having us break into pairs or small groups for discussions, which made it much easier for me to open up. Now, I feel much more comfortable sharing with the whole group."

Establishing ground rules for respectful communication is essential for maintaining a positive and supportive atmosphere. These rules might include guidelines about confidentiality, respectful disagreement, and refraining from unsolicited advice.

John, a long-time member of a grandparent group, explains: "We have a few simple rules that everyone agrees to when they join. Things like keeping what's shared in the group confidential, avoiding judgmental language, and respecting different parenting and grandparenting styles. These rules help everyone feel safe to share openly."

Planning Engaging Activities

While simply coming together to chat can be valuable, planning specific activities can enhance your gatherings and provide structure and focus. These activities can cater to various interests and needs within the group, ensuring that meetings remain fresh and engaging.

Inviting guest speakers on relevant topics can be an excellent way to provide valuable information and spark discussions. Topics might include child development, modern parenting trends, technology, and children or legal issues affecting grandparents.

James, a member of a grandparent group, shares: "One of our most popular meetings was when we had a local pediatrician come to speak about current health recommendations for children. It was fascinating to learn how much has changed since we raised our own kids, and it sparked great discussions."

This type of expert input can be particularly valuable in helping grandparents stay informed about current best practices in childcare and development. It also provides a common base of knowledge for the group to discuss and apply to their own situations.

Craft sessions for making gifts for grandchildren can be both fun and practical. These sessions allow grandparents to create personalized presents while enjoying social time with peers. Activities might include knitting, scrapbooking, or creating custom storybooks.

Mary, a grandmother of four, enjoys these sessions: "We had a workshop on making personalized story cubes. It was so much fun, and now I have a unique gift for each of my grandchildren. Plus, I learned a new craft that I can do with them when they visit."

Book club discussions on grandparenting books can provide a structured way to explore various aspects of the grandparent role. This activity combines learning with social interaction and can lead to deep, meaningful conversations about the joys and challenges of grandparenting.

Linda, an avid reader, started a book club within her grandparent group: "We meet every other month to discuss a book related to grandparenting. It's wonderful to get different perspectives on the ideas in the books, and it often leads to sharing our own experiences. I've learned so much from these discussions."

Skill-sharing workshops where grandparents teach each other their talents can be a great way to leverage the diverse skills within the group. This might include sessions on gardening, basic home repairs, using smartphones effectively, or cooking family recipes.

Organizing Multigenerational Events

While grandparent-only gatherings are important, organizing events that include grandchildren can be a wonderful way to build community and create shared experiences. These multigenerational events allow grandparents to interact with their peers while also spending quality time with their grandchildren.

Expert M.A.B. (2018) suggests planning for three-hour playdates with grandchildren, which could be adapted for group settings (Expert M.A.B., 2018). This timeframe is long enough for meaningful activities but not so long that it becomes overwhelming for children or grandparents.

Park playdates are a simple yet effective multigenerational event. They provide a casual setting for grandparents to socialize while children play. These events can be enhanced with organized games or nature-based activities.

Emma, a grandmother of two, shares her experience: "We organize monthly 'Grandparents and Grands Park Days.' We choose a different local park each time, and it's wonderful to see the children playing together while our grandparents catch up. We usually bring some outdoor games like giant Jenga or parachute games that everyone can enjoy together."

Holiday parties can be festive multigenerational gatherings. These events can incorporate holiday-themed crafts, storytelling, or cultural traditions, providing an opportunity for grandparents to pass on family and cultural heritage.

David, a grandfather of three, recalls a successful holiday event: "Last December, we had a 'Grandparents and Grandkids Holiday Cookie Bake.' Each family brought a traditional holiday cookie recipe to share. The kids had a blast decorating cookies, and we grandparents enjoyed exchanging family stories and traditions. It was a beautiful way to celebrate the season together."

Intergenerational craft workshops can be both fun and educational. These might include activities like creating family trees, making memory books, or working on simple woodworking projects together.

Margaret, a grandmother of three, recalls a successful event: "We organized a 'Grandparents and Grandkids Baking Day' at a local community center. Each grandparent-grandchild pair made a family recipe together. The kids loved it, and we grandparents got to chat while we baked. It was chaotic but so much fun, and we all went home with delicious treats."

Storytelling sessions where grandparents share family histories can be a powerful way to connect generations. These events can be themed around topics like childhood memories, family traditions, or historical events lived through.

George, a grandfather known for his storytelling, shares: "We had a 'Family History Day' where grandparents brought old photos and shared stories about their childhoods. The grandkids were fascinated, asking questions and comparing their lives to ours. It was a wonderful way to pass on family history and create new memories at the same time."

These multigenerational events not only provide enjoyable experiences but also strengthen the bonds between grandparents and grandchildren. They offer opportunities for grandparents to model positive social interactions and for grandchildren to develop relationships with their peers in a family-oriented setting.

When organizing these events, it's important to consider the needs of both generations. Ensure there are comfortable seating areas for grandparents, safe play spaces for children, and activities that can engage both age groups. It's also helpful to have a few volunteers to assist with managing activities and ensuring everyone's comfort and safety.

Chapter 8:

Leaving a Legacy

As grandparents, we have a unique opportunity to leave a lasting impact on our grandchildren and future generations. This chapter explores the importance of creating a meaningful legacy, focusing on how we can pass down family traditions, impart valuable life lessons, and create enduring memories. By understanding our role in shaping the future, we can ensure that our wisdom, values, and love continue to influence our families long after we're gone.

The Importance of Family Traditions and Tales

Family traditions and stories are the threads that weave together the fabric of our family history. They provide a sense of identity, continuity, and belonging for our grandchildren. As sunshineretirementliving (2016) points out, "Family traditions are how we pass down beliefs and values, build strong relationships, and create lasting memories" (sunshineretirementliving, 2016).

These traditions and tales serve multiple purposes in strengthening family bonds and shaping the character of younger generations. They offer a connection to the past, helping grandchildren understand their roots and the journey their family has taken.

This understanding can foster a sense of pride and belonging, giving children a strong foundation as they navigate their own lives.

Margaret, a grandmother of four, shares her experience: "Every Thanksgiving, I gather my grandchildren around the kitchen table to make our family's secret recipe apple pie. As we peel apples and roll out dough, I tell them stories about their great-grandmother, who created the recipe during the Great Depression. It's more than just baking; it's a way to connect them to their roots and teach them about resilience and creativity."

This simple tradition not only creates a delicious dessert but also serves as a vehicle for passing down family history and values. It gives the grandchildren a tangible connection to their ancestors and helps them understand where they come from. The act of baking together creates a shared experience that strengthens family bonds, while the stories shared during the process impart important life lessons about perseverance and adaptability.

Margaret's tradition also demonstrates how everyday activities can be transformed into meaningful rituals that children look forward to year after year. The anticipation and repetition of these traditions create a sense of stability and continuity in children's lives, which is particularly valuable in today's fast-paced and often unpredictable world.

Creating Family History Books and Videos

In today's digital age, we have numerous tools at our disposal to preserve and share our family history. Creating family history books or videos can be a meaningful way to document your family's journey for future generations. These records serve as tangible links to the past, allowing future generations to connect with their ancestors in a profound way. Chip (2023) suggests, "Preserving and passing down family stories is crucial for maintaining family identity and unity across generations" (Chip, 2023). This process can be as simple or as elaborate as you choose, from handwritten journals to professionally produced documentaries. The key is to capture the essence of your family's story in a way that will resonate with future generations.

Robert, a tech-savvy grandfather, shares his approach: "I started a digital family archive using a cloud storage service. I scan old photos, record video interviews with family members, and even create short documentaries about significant family events. My grandkids love watching videos of their parents as children, and it's sparked their interest in our family history."

Robert's method showcases how modern technology can be harnessed to preserve and share family history in engaging ways. By digitizing old photographs and documents, he's ensuring that these precious memories are protected from physical deterioration. The video interviews he conducts capture not just the words but also the voices, expressions, and personalities of family members, providing a rich, multidimensional record for future generations.

When creating these historical records, it's important to include a variety of elements to paint a comprehensive picture of your family's story. Family tree information provides the structural backbone of your history, showing how different family members are related and how the family has grown over time. Old photographs with detailed captions bring the past to life, allowing future generations to see the faces of their ancestors and understand the contexts of their lives.

Personal anecdotes and memories add color and emotion to your family history. These stories, whether they're tales of triumph over adversity, funny mishaps, or everyday life in a different era, help humanize your ancestors and make their experiences relatable to future generations. Including historical context for significant family events helps place your family's story within the broader sweep of history, showing how world events shaped your family's journey. Family recipes and traditions are also valuable inclusions in any family history project. These tangible links to the past can be recreated by future generations, allowing them to literally taste their heritage or participate in activities that their ancestors enjoyed.

Remember, the goal is not just to record facts but to tell the story of your family in a way that engages and inspires future generations. This means going beyond names and dates to capture the personalities, values, and experiences that have shaped your family over time.

Examples of Meaningful Family Legacies

Family legacies can take many forms, from tangible heirlooms to shared values and experiences. The most meaningful legacies are often those that reflect the unique character and history of your family. These legacies serve as bridges between generations, allowing grandparents to pass on not just objects but also skills, values, and a sense of family identity.

Sarah, a grandmother of three, created a unique legacy: "I started a family quilt project. Each year, I add a new square representing a significant family event. I involve my grandchildren in choosing the designs and fabrics. It's become a visual representation of our family's journey, and my grandchildren love pointing out the squares that represent their births or special achievements."

Sarah's quilt project is a beautiful example of a legacy that combines a tangible object with shared experiences and family history. The quilt itself is a physical representation of the family's journey, with each square telling a story. By involving her grandchildren in the process of choosing designs and fabrics, Sarah is not only creating a family heirloom but also teaching them about the significant events in their family's history. This collaborative process strengthens family bonds and gives the grandchildren a sense of ownership in their family's legacy.

The quilt also serves as a conversation starter, encouraging discussion about family history and values. As the grandchildren grow older, the quilt can be used to remind them of their family's journey and the important events that have shaped their lives. It's a legacy that will continue to grow and evolve with the family, potentially being passed down through multiple generations.

Another example comes from James, a grandfather with a passion for woodworking: "I've been teaching my grandchildren how to work with wood. We're building a dollhouse together, and I'm using it as an opportunity to pass down not just skills but also values like patience, attention to detail, and the satisfaction of creating something with your own hands."

James's legacy is primarily one of shared experiences and skills, with the dollhouse serving as a physical representation of these lessons. By working together on this project, James is creating lasting memories with his grandchildren while also teaching them valuable skills. The process of building the dollhouse provides numerous opportunities to impart life lessons, from the importance of planning and perseverance to the value of craftsmanship and creativity.

Moreover, the dollhouse itself will serve as a lasting reminder of the time spent with their grandfather and the lessons learned. It's a tangible symbol of their shared experiences that the grandchildren can keep and potentially pass on to their own children one day. These examples show how legacies can be both tangible and intangible, combining physical objects with the transmission of skills, values, and shared experiences. The most powerful legacies often intertwine these elements, creating multi-faceted connections between generations. For instance, a family might pass down a collection of letters written by an ancestor, along with the value of maintaining close family connections despite distance. Or a grandmother might teach her grandchildren to cook traditional family recipes, passing on both culinary skills and cultural heritage.

The key to creating meaningful family legacies is to identify what is unique and important about your family's history, values, and talents and find ways to pass these on to future generations. This might involve creating new traditions, sharing skills, preserving family stories, or passing down meaningful objects. The most important aspect is that these legacies resonate with your family's identity and values, creating a lasting connection between past, present, and future generations.

Teaching Values and Life Lessons

The Role of Grandparents in Imparting Wisdom

Grandparents play a crucial role in imparting wisdom and values to younger generations. As Mckeown (2023) notes, "Grandparents often have the time, patience, and life experience to teach and impart wisdom in a way that parents may not always be able to" (Mckeown, 2023). This unique position allows grandparents to serve as mentors, confidants, and guides for their grandchildren.

The role of grandparents in a child's life is multifaceted and profoundly influential. Unlike parents, who are often caught up in the day-to-day responsibilities of raising children, grandparents can offer a different perspective, one that comes from years of life experience and the ability to see the bigger picture. This vantage point allows them to impart wisdom in a way that can be both impactful and long-lasting.

Grandparents often have more time to spend with their grandchildren, allowing for deeper conversations and more opportunities to share life lessons. This unhurried time can create a safe space for grandchildren to ask questions, express doubts, and seek guidance. The relaxed nature of the grandparent-grandchild relationship can make it easier for children to open up and be receptive to the wisdom being shared.

Moreover, grandparents bring a historical perspective that can be invaluable in helping grandchildren understand their place in the world. They can share stories about family history, cultural traditions, and societal changes they've witnessed over their lifetime. This connection to the past can help children develop a stronger sense of identity and belonging.

Emma Reed (2024) emphasizes, "Learning from grandparents is a source of wisdom and inspiration that can shape a child's character and worldview" (Reed 2024). This underscores the profound impact we can have on our grandchildren's development. The values, beliefs, and life lessons imparted by grandparents can shape a child's moral compass and influence their decisions well into adulthood.

By sharing our life experiences, both successes and failures, we can provide valuable insights and help our grandchildren navigate life's challenges. Our stories of overcoming adversity, learning from mistakes, and achieving goals can serve as powerful teaching tools. These personal anecdotes make abstract concepts like perseverance, integrity, and compassion more tangible and relatable for young minds.

Methods for Imparting Life Lessons

There are many ways to impart valuable life lessons to our grandchildren. The key is to find methods that resonate with both the grandparent and the grandchild, creating meaningful interactions that foster learning and growth.

Storytelling is one of the most powerful methods, allowing us to share our experiences in a relatable and engaging way. Stories have a unique ability to capture attention, evoke emotions, and make complex ideas more accessible. When we share stories from our own lives, we not only impart wisdom but also deepen our connection with our grandchildren.

Thomas, a grandfather of five, shares his approach: "I keep a 'wisdom journal' where I write down life lessons I've learned. When my grandchildren face challenges or have questions about life, I refer to this journal to share relevant stories and advice. It helps me organize my thoughts and ensures I'm passing on the most important lessons I've learned."

Thomas's method is particularly effective because it allows him to reflect on his experiences and distill them into clear lessons. By writing down these insights, he ensures that important life lessons aren't forgotten or overlooked. The journal also serves as a tangible legacy that his grandchildren can refer to even when he's not around.

Another effective method is leading by example. Our actions often speak louder than words, and grandchildren are keen observers of how we handle situations and treat others. By embodying the values we wish to instill, we provide a living example for our grandchildren to emulate.

Linda, a grandmother known for her volunteer work, explains: "I started taking my grandchildren with me to volunteer at the local food bank. It's been a wonderful way to teach them about compassion, community service, and gratitude. Seeing the impact of our work firsthand has made these values come alive for them in a way that simply talking about it never could."

Linda's approach demonstrates how hands-on experiences can be powerful teaching tools. By involving her grandchildren in her volunteer work, she's not just telling them about the importance of helping others – she's showing them. This experiential learning creates lasting memories and deep-seated values that are likely to stay with her grandchildren throughout their lives.

Other methods for imparting life lessons include:

- **Open discussions:** Creating an environment where grandchildren feel comfortable asking questions and expressing their thoughts can lead to meaningful conversations about life, values, and ethics.

- **Shared activities:** Engaging in hobbies or activities together provides opportunities to teach skills, patience, and the value of practice and perseverance.

- **Reading together:** Books can be excellent springboards for discussions about values, choices, and life lessons.

- **Teaching family traditions:** Passing down family traditions can instill a sense of identity and values associated with your family's culture and history.

- **Problem-solving together:** Helping grandchildren work through challenges can teach critical thinking, resilience, and the importance of not giving up.

The most effective approach often involves a combination of these methods tailored to the age, interests, and personality of each grandchild. The key is to make the process of learning values and life lessons an engaging and positive experience.

Stories of Influential Grandparents

Throughout history, many influential figures have credited their grandparents with shaping their character and values. These stories can inspire us in our own grandparenting journey, showing the profound and lasting impact we can have on our grandchildren's lives.

One famous example is Maya Angelou, who was raised by her grandmother for several years. Angelou often spoke about how her grandmother's strength, dignity, and faith profoundly influenced her life and work. In her writings, Angelou described her grandmother as a pillar of strength in the community, a woman who faced racial discrimination with unwavering dignity and taught young Maya the power of self-respect and perseverance.

Angelou's grandmother, Annie Henderson, ran a successful store during the Great Depression and was known for her generosity to those in need. This example of entrepreneurship and community service left a lasting impression on Angelou, influencing her own approach to life and her commitment to social justice.

Another notable example is former U.S. President Barack Obama, who was largely raised by his maternal grandparents. Obama has often spoken about the influence his grandmother, Madelyn Dunham, had on his life. He credits her with instilling in him the values of hard work, education, and financial responsibility. Her support and belief in his potential played a crucial role in shaping his character and ambitions.

On a more personal level, Maria, now a grandmother herself, shares: "My grandfather was a Holocaust survivor. He taught me about resilience, the importance of education, and standing up against injustice. His stories and lessons have shaped my life, and now I'm passing those same values on to my grandchildren. It's a living legacy that spans generations."

Maria's story illustrates how the profound experiences of one generation can shape the values and worldview of subsequent generations. Her grandfather's survival of one of history's darkest periods and his ability to rebuild his life afterward provided powerful lessons in resilience and the triumph of the human spirit. By sharing these stories and lessons with her grandchildren, Maria is ensuring that her grandfather's wisdom and the values he held dear continue to influence future generations.

These stories highlight the lasting impact grandparents can have, influencing not just their immediate family but potentially society at large through the values they instill in younger generations. They demonstrate how the love, wisdom, and experiences of grandparents can shape the character, ambitions, and worldview of their grandchildren in profound and enduring ways.

The influence of grandparents often extends far beyond childhood, continuing to guide and inspire their grandchildren well into adulthood. Many successful individuals attribute their achievements and values to the early influence of their grandparents, showing how the seeds planted in childhood can bear fruit throughout a person's life.

As grandparents, we have the opportunity to create our own stories of influence tailored to our unique experiences, values, and the needs of our grandchildren. Whether through daily interactions, special traditions, or the overall example we set, we have the power to shape the future by influencing the characters and values of the next generation.

Creating Lasting Memories

The Value of Shared Experiences

Creating lasting memories through shared experiences is one of the most precious gifts we can give our grandchildren. As Drjuneau (2016) points out, "Experiences create the most amazing memories, fostering emotional connections that last a lifetime" (Dr Juneau, 2016).

These shared experiences don't have to be grand or expensive. Often, it's the simple, heartfelt moments that leave the most lasting impressions. The key is to be fully present and engaged at the moment, creating an atmosphere of love, fun, and connection.

Suggestions for Unique Excursions and Pastimes

While everyday interactions are important, planning special outings or activities can create particularly memorable experiences. Here are some ideas to consider:

- **Nature adventures:** Plan hiking trips, camping weekends, or even backyard explorations to foster a love for nature and outdoor activities.

- **Cultural experiences:** Visit museums, attend concerts or plays, or explore different cultural festivals to broaden your grandchildren's horizons.

- **Skill-sharing sessions:** Teach your grandchildren skills you've mastered, whether it's cooking, gardening, painting, or a craft.

- **Travel experiences:** If possible, plan trips together, even if they're just short local getaways. Traveling creates unique bonding opportunities and exposes children to new experiences.

- **Community service:** Engage in volunteer activities together, teaching the value of giving back to the community.

Carol, a grandmother of three, shares her experience: "Every summer, I take each of my grandchildren on a special 'grandma camp' weekend. We choose a nearby destination, and I plan activities around their interests. My eldest granddaughter and I went on a fossil-hunting trip last year. She still talks about the ammonite we found together. These one-on-one trips have become cherished traditions that we all look forward to."

The Impact on Growth and Emotions

These shared experiences have a profound impact on both the emotional and personal growth of our grandchildren. They provide opportunities for learning, building self-confidence, and strengthening family bonds.

Alia Siddique (2023) notes, "Grandparents play a crucial role in a child's emotional development, offering a unique form of love and support" (Siddique, 2023). The memories created through shared experiences become emotional anchors, providing comfort and inspiration throughout our grandchildren's lives.

David, a grandfather of four, reflects on the impact of his efforts: "I've been taking my grandkids stargazing since they were little. At first, it was just about the excitement of staying up late and using the telescope. But over the years, it's led to deep conversations about the universe, our place in it, and the importance of wonder and curiosity. I've seen how these experiences have sparked their interest in science and fostered a sense of awe about the world. It's amazing to see how a simple activity can have such a profound influence on their development."

Conclusion

As we reach the end of our journey through "Navigating the first year as a modern grandparent: A comprehensive guide," it's time to reflect on the wealth of knowledge we've explored together. This book has aimed to equip you with the tools, insights, and encouragement needed to embrace your role as a grandparent in today's dynamic world.

We began by discussing the importance of embracing your new role, setting realistic expectations, and finding your unique grandparenting style. Remember, this transformation brings both joy and challenges, and it's crucial to approach it with an open mind and heart.

Building strong relationships with your grandchildren was a key focus. We emphasized creating memorable moments, understanding the value of playtime, and fostering a bond that will grow and evolve. These early interactions are the foundation of a lifelong connection that will bring immense joy and fulfillment to both you and your grandchildren.

In our rapidly changing society, staying informed about modern parenting trends is essential. We explored updates on health and safety guidelines, various parenting philosophies, and the importance of supporting your adult children in their parenting journey. This knowledge will help you navigate the sometimes tricky waters of intergenerational relationships while ensuring the well-being of your grandchildren.

For those facing the challenges of long-distance grandparenting, we provided strategies for maintaining strong connections through virtual means and creative communication methods. Remember, geographical distance doesn't have to equate to emotional distance. With effort and creativity, you can maintain a close and loving relationship with your grandchildren, no matter where you are.

Balancing your grandparenting role with your personal life emerged as a crucial theme. We stressed the importance of maintaining your interests, setting healthy boundaries, and taking care of your physical and emotional well-being. By doing so, you can be a more effective, fulfilled, and present grandparent.

Supporting new parents was another key focus. We highlighted the need to honor parental decisions while offering practical and emotional support. We learned that open and honest communication is the cornerstone of a harmonious family dynamic. Your role as a supportive, respectful presence can make a world of difference to overwhelmed new parents.

We explored the benefits of establishing a network of grandparents, encouraging you to connect with others on a similar journey. Sharing resources, experiences, and wisdom can greatly enrich your grandparenting experience and provide a valuable support system.

Finally, we discussed the profound impact you can have by leaving a lasting legacy. By passing down family traditions, imparting valuable life lessons, and creating enduring memories, you have the power to influence generations to come. Your stories, values, and love will live on through your grandchildren and beyond.

As you embark on this grandparenting journey, remember that there's no one "right" way to be a grandparent. Your relationship with your grandchildren will be as unique as you are. This guide is not about perfection but about helping you become the best grandparent you can be.

We encourage you to put the knowledge and strategies you've gained from this book into practice. Start by choosing one or two areas where you'd like to focus your efforts. Perhaps you'll initiate a new family tradition, or maybe you'll explore ways to better support the new parents in your life. Whatever you choose, take that first step with confidence.

Remember to be patient with yourself and others as you navigate this new role. Grandparenting, like any relationship, is a journey of continuous learning and growth. Don't be afraid to make mistakes – they're often our best teachers.

We also encourage you to stay connected with other grandparents. Consider joining a local grandparent group or participating in online communities. Sharing your experiences and learning from others can be incredibly rewarding and supportive.

As you move forward, keep in mind that your role as a grandparent is invaluable. You have the power to provide love, support, wisdom, and a sense of family heritage to your grandchildren. Your presence in their lives is a gift that will continue to impact them long into the future.

We hope this book has provided you with the knowledge, tools, and inspiration to fully embrace your role as a modern grandparent. May your grandparenting journey be filled with love, laughter, and countless precious moments.

Remember, the adventure is just beginning. Embrace it with an open heart, a willing spirit, and the wisdom you've gained. Your grandchildren – and your entire family – will be richer for it.

As a call to action, we encourage you to start implementing the strategies you've learned. Choose one aspect of grandparenting you'd like to improve and set a concrete goal for the coming week. Whether it's planning a special activity with your grandchild, having a heart-to-heart with your adult child, or connecting with other grandparents, take that first step today.

Lastly, if you've found this book helpful, consider sharing your experiences with other grandparents. Your journey could inspire and guide others who are just beginning their grandparenting adventure.

Happy grandparenting! The best is yet to come.

Glossary

Attachment Parenting: A parenting philosophy emphasizing physical and emotional closeness between parents and children.

Baby-led Weaning: **A method of introducing solid foods that allow babies to feed** themselves from the start of weaning.

Babywearing: The practice of carrying a baby in a sling or carrier close to the body.

Boundaries: Limits set in relationships to maintain healthy interactions and respect personal space.

Care Packages: Parcels sent to loved ones containing gifts, treats, or necessities, often used in long-distance relationships.

Co-sleeping: The practice of parents sleeping close to their child, often in the same bed.

Digital Parenting Tools: Apps and online resources designed to assist parents in tracking and managing childcare tasks.

Extended Breastfeeding: Continuing to breastfeed beyond infancy, often into toddlerhood or beyond.

Family Heritage: The history, traditions, and cultural background of a family passed down through generations.

Family Legacy: The passing down of values, traditions, and memories from one generation to another.

Gentle Parenting: A parenting approach that emphasizes empathy, respect, and understanding in child-rearing.

Grandparent Burnout: A state of physical, emotional, and mental exhaustion that can occur from the demands of grandparenting.

Grandparent Classes: Educational sessions designed to help grandparents understand modern parenting practices and their role.

Grandparent Network: A support system of fellow grandparents who share experiences and advice.

Intergenerational Activities: Events or pastimes that involve and appeal to multiple generations.

Long-distance Grandparenting: Maintaining a relationship with grandchildren who live far away, often using technology to stay connected.

Mindfulness: The practice of being fully present and engaged in the current moment.

Modern Parenting Trends: Contemporary approaches to child-rearing, often influenced by recent research and societal changes.

Montessori Parenting: An approach based on the educational philosophy of Maria Montessori, emphasizing independence and natural development in children.

Multigenerational Events: Gatherings or activities that involve multiple generations of a family.

NICU: Neonatal Intensive Care Unit, a specialized unit for newborns needing intensive medical care.

Online Communities: Virtual groups where people with common interests or experiences can connect and share information.

Positive Parenting: A parenting approach that focuses on positive reinforcement and building a strong parent-child relationship.

Positive Discipline: A method of correcting behavior that focuses on teaching rather than punishment.

References

8 Tips for Long-Distance Grandparents. (n.d.). Sedgebrook. https://www.welcometosedgebrook.com/blog/tips-for-long-distance-grandparents/

9 Parenting Trends That Today's Grandparents Just Don't Understand. (2019, February 11). Woman's World. https://www.womansworld.com/posts/family/parenting-trends-grandparents-don-t-understand-157191 13

13 Fun Things to do with Grandparents and Grandchildren. (2024, February 6). Age Co. https://www.ageukmobility.co.uk/mobility-news/article/grandparent-and-grandchildren-activity-ideas#:~:text=One%2Don%2Done%20interaction%20and

80 Best Grandparent Blogs and Websites in 2024. (2024, July 10). FeedSpot. https://family.feedspot.com/grandparent_blogs/ A Care Package Saves a Life...Again. (2012, May 21).

Operation Gratitude. https://opgrat.wordpress.com/2012/05/21/a-care-package-saves-a-life-again/

Bell, J. (2024, February 19). What Now?. Christian Grandparenting. https://christiangrandparenting.com/now-that-youre-a-grandparent/

Borresen, K. (2024, February 28). Here's What Grandparents Really Think About Today's Parenting Trends. Huffington Post. https://www.huffpost.com/entry/grandparents-weigh-in-todays-parenting-trends_l_65d791fbe4b0189a6a7d3e9d

Build Traditions with Your Grandchildren. (2017, July 17). GaGa Sisterhoodd. https://www.gagasisterhood.com/2017/build-traditions-with-your-grandchildren/

Burke, M. A. (n.d.). The Three Hour Grandma Play Dates!. GenParenting. https://genparenting.com/3-hour-play-dates-with-grandkids/

Canfield, K. (2020, January 16). Granparenting: Magical Connections and Very Real Benefits. Grandkids Matter. https://grandkidsmatter.org/hot-topics/grandchildren/grandparenting-magical-connections-very-real-benefits/

Care Packages and Correspondence Research: History and Tips. (2019, September 27). Badges for All. https://badgesforall.wordpress.com/2019/09/27/care-packages-and-correspondence-research-history-and-tips/

Condie, K. (2023, November 3). Grandparenting: A Balancing Act. Growing Faith. https://growingfaith.com.au/articles/grandparenting-a-balancing-act

Dwyer, L. (2023, November 6). 10 Ways New Grandparents Can Start Off on the Right Foot. The Bump. https://www.thebump.com/a/new-grandparent-tips.

Ebisujima, J. (n.d.). How to Identify and Ebrace Your Montessori Parenting Style. Jojoebi. https://www.jojoebi.com/how-to-identify-and-embrace-your-montessori-parenting-style/

Feister, J. (2019, August 21). Long-distance Grandparenting is Not Easy. Here's How These Families Make it Work. America Magazine. https://www.americamagazine.org/faith/2019/08/21/long-distance-grandparenting-not-easy-heres-how-these-families-make-it-work.

Finn, C. (2022, March 1). Jan's Family Traditions and How to Create Your Own. The DIY Playbook. https://thediyplaybook.com/how-to-create-family-traditions/

Garlinge, K. (n.d.). What's the Best Type of Parenting Style of Philosophy for You?. Lovevery. https://lovevery.com/community/blog/podcast/whats-the-best-type-of-parenting-style-of-philosophy-for-you

Grandparents: Getting The Best From Your Parents and In-Laws. (n.d.). NCT. https://www.nct.org.uk/life-parent/grandparents/grandparents-getting-best-your-parents-and-laws.

How to Avoid Grandparent Burnout and Other Perils of Looking After Grandkids. (2023, February 1). More than Grand.

https://www.morethangrand.com/blog/how-to-avoid-grandparent-burnout#:~:text=Grandparents%20caring%20for%20their%20grandchildren

How To Bond With Your Grandchildren At Every Stage of Their Lives. (2023, January 30). Devoted Grandma. https://www.devotedgrandma.com/grandparenting/bonding-with-grandkids/

Involved Grandparenting and Life Balance. (2024, January 17). Grandkids Matter. https://grandkidsmatter.org/hot-topics/parents/involved-grandparenting-and-life-balance/

Is Your Grandchild in the NICU? Here's How You Can Help. (2013, May 27). Hand to Hold. https://handtohold.org/when-your-grandchild-in-the-nicu-helping-grandparents-understand-and-help/

Jacobs, C. (2017, June 20). Pursuing Healthy Relationships with Grandchildren. Grandkids Matter. https://grandkidsmatter.org/hot-topics/grandchildren/pursuing-healthy-relationships-with-grandchildren/

Kemp, G., Segal, J., Robinson, L., & Reid, S. (2024, June 4). Grandparenting Tips: How tot be a Better Grandparent. HelpGuide. https://www.helpguide.org/articles/parenting-family/grandparenting-tips-how-to-be-a-better-grandparent.htm.

Kimerer, K. (2023, November 13). Standing Out with Physical Mail. Mailing Technology. https://mailingsystemstechnology.com/article-5155-Standing-Out-with-Physical-Mail.html

Landsem, I. P., & Cheetham, N. B. (2022, September 8). Infant Sleep as a Topic in Healthcare Guidance of Parents, Prenatally and the First 6 Months After Birth: A Scoping Review. BMC Health Services. https://doi.org/10.1186/s12913-022-08484-3.

Lansbury, J. (n.d.). Dealing With Parenting Diffferences Among Friends, Family and Kind Strangers. Janet Lansbury Elevating Child Care. https://www.janetlansbury.com/2011/03/dealing-with-parenting-differences-among-friends-family-and-kind-strangers/.

Letter Printing and Mailing Services: Modernizing Traditional Marketing. (2024, May 9). FSSI. https://www.fssi-ca.com/the-power-of-letter-printing-and-mailing-modernizing-tradition

Lund, D. (2017, November 11). A Health Child Gets Ample Sleep, Nutrition, and Activity. Sanford Health. https://news.sanfordhealth.org/childrens/healthy-child-gets-ample-sleep-nutrition-activity/.

Macias, S. (2022, April 27). 5 Traditions to Start with Grandchildren for Making Lifelong Memories. The Joyful Life. https://joyfullifemagazine.com/traditions-to-start-with-grandchildren/

Nkala, D. N. (2024, April 15). Outsourced Parenting: Is Technology Raising Our Children?. Linkedin. https://www.linkedin.com/pulse/outsourced-parenting-technology-raising-our-children-part-nkala-yi2cf/.

Practical Advice for Granparents From a New Mom. (2022, November 22). Daily Magic. https://dailymagicatl.com/2022/11/22/practical-advice-for-grandparents-from-a-new-mom/

Relationships and Child Development. (2023, March 22). Raising Children - The Australian Parenting Site. https://raisingchildren.net.au/newborns/development/understanding-development/relationships-development

Robbins, J. (n.d.). Why Experiences Create the Most Amazing Memories. Dr. Juneau Robbins. https://drjuneaurobbins.com/experiences-make-memories/

Rumbaugh, P. (n.d.). 5 Suggestions for Grandparents and Grandkids to Have Fun Together. The Genius of Play. https://thegeniusofplay.org/genius/expert-advice/articles/5-suggestions-for-grandparents-and-grandkids-to-have-fun-together.aspx

Savage, J. (n.d.). How to Bond With Your Grandkisd. Focus on the Family. https://www.focusonthefamily.com/parenting/a-grand-influence-how-to-bond-with-your-grandkids/

Setting Boundaries with Adult Children and Grandchildren. (2024, July 12). Compass. https://www.compass.info/featured-topics/family-relationships/setting-boundaries-with-adult-children-and-grandchildren/

Siddique, A. (n.d.). Importance of Granparents in Parenting: 10 Vital Roles They Play for Kids!. Mind Family. https://mind.family/articles/importance-of-grandparents-in-parenting/

Tuckova, M. (n.d.). Montessori Parenting int he 21st Century. Montessori Parenting. https://montessoriparenting.org/montessori-parenting-in-the-21st-century-part-2/

Why Grandparents Don't Respect Boundaries. (2023, January 1). More than Grand. https://www.morethangrand.com/blog/why-grandparents-dont-respect-boundaries

Printed in Great Britain
by Amazon